easy slow cooker

easy slow cooker

fuss-free family food from your slow cooker

RYLAND PETERS & SMALL
LONDON • NEW YORK

Senior Designer Toni Kay
Commissioning Editor Julia Charles
Picture Research Emily Westlake
Production Gordana Simakovic
Art Director Leslie Harrington
Publishing Director Alison Starling

Indexer Hilary Bird
Recipe Testing and Adaptation
  Not Just Food Ltd

Originally published as separate UK
and US editions in 2010. This revised
dual edition published in 2018 by
Ryland Peters & Small
20–21 Jockey's Fields
London WC1R 4BW
and
341 E 116th St
New York NY 10029

www.rylandpeters.com

Design and commissioned photographs
© Ryland Peters & Small 2010, 2018.

Text © Ghillie Basan, Fiona Beckett,
Tessa Bramley, Maxine Clark, Ross Dobson,
Ursula Ferrigno, Silvana Franco, Liz Franklin,
Manisha Gambhir Harkins, Tonia George, Brian
Glover, Clare Gordon-Smith, Rachael Anne Hill,
Jennifer Joyce, Caroline Marson, Fiona Smith,
Sonia Stevenson, Sunil Vijayakar, Fran Warde,
Laura Washburn, Lindy Wildsmith, and Ryland
Peters & Small 2010, 2018.

ISBN: 978-1-84975-913-7

NOTES

* Both British (Metric) and American (Imperial
plus US cup) measurements are included in these
recipes for your convenience, however it is
important to work with one set of measurements
and not alternate between the two within a recipe

* All spoon measurements are level unless
otherwise specified. A teaspoon is 5 ml and
a tablespoon is 15 ml.

* Read your slow cooker manual before you begin
and preheat the slow cooker if required according
to the manufacturer's instructions. Because slow
cookers vary slightly from manufacturer to
manufacturer, always check recipe timings with
your model's directions for a recipe using the same
ingredients.

* Where a recipe is finished off under the
grill/broiler, hold the dish with kitchen cloths to
remove it from the machine.

contents

slow cooker know-how

Slow cookers are electrical appliances with a metal outer sleeve containing an element and a ceramic cooking pot which sits on top of the element with a lid. (They are often referred to as Crock Pots as a generic name, as this is one of the most widely used brands in the USA.) They cook food at relatively low temperatures compared to other popular cooking methods and are very energy-efficient, using up to 80 per cent less energy than conventional ovens. Slow cookers are useful for busy lifestyles – with as little as 15–20 minutes' preparation time, they can be set up to cook a meal ready for the evening and left on safely while you are out. Slow cookers are designed for moist-heat cooking where moisture in the food condenses on the lid and drops back into the pot, making it a great cooking method for soups and casseroles. In addition, the slow-cooking process can make cheaper cuts of meat tender by cooking them over low heat for several hours, a boon for any cook managing a household budget.

choosing which slow cooker to buy

You can buy around four different sizes of slow cooker, the total capacity and working capacity of which will be printed on the packaging. The working capacity means the maximum space for food.

- **For two people**, go for a mini cooker with a total capacity of 1.5 litres/quarts of which the working capacity is 1 litres/quart.

- **For four people**, pick a cooker with a total capacity of 3–5 litres/quarts giving you a working capacity of 2.5 litres/quarts.

- **For six people**, choose a 5-litre/
  -quart capacity cooker with a
  working capacity of 4 litres/quarts.

- **For six to eight people**, look for
  a 6.5-litre/quart capacity cooker
  with a working capacity of
  4.5 litres/quarts.

- **For an average family**, the four
  person capacity cooker should suit
  well. Only choose the very large
  model if you intend on making
  extra to freeze regularly or you
  have many mouths to feed. In all
  sizes, you will find round or oval
  cookers. The oval is most versatile
  and best for a baking dish, whole
  chicken or a joint of meat.

caring for a slow cooker

After cooking in your slow cooker,
make sure it is completely cool before
attempting to clean it. Unplug it from
the mains and remove the ceramic pot.
This will be removable in most makes
of slow cooker. Wipe the base unit with
a warm, damp cloth and dry with a
kitchen cloth or paper towels. Be
mindful of the fact that the cooker
has an electrical plug and lead which
should be kept dry at all times.

Wash the ceramic pot and lid in
warm soapy water, making sure to
remove any pieces of food from the
vent in the lid and around the edges.
Soaking is an effective way to remove
any cooked-on food but do not leave
the cooking pot immersed in the sink;
just fill with warm soapy water and
let soak until the cooked-on food
comes away freely. (Some models
feature dishwasher-safe pots so check
your manual.) Pack your slow cooker
away only when it is completely cool,
clean and thoroughly dry.

TIP

Your slow cooker is an invaluable
way to use up leftovers too. Odds and
ends of vegetables make a great soup,
or add pulses/legumes and leftover
cooked meats for an economical meal.

getting started

It is exciting using a piece of kitchen equipment for the first time. Take your time and don't rush into cooking anything until you have read the instruction manual thoroughly. It may take a little time to get used to using a slow cooker as it can be quite different from other cooking methods. After unpacking your new slow cooker, make sure you wash the inner ceramic pot and the lid with warm soapy water. Dry thoroughly. Find a position in your kitchen where the slow cooker will be safe. Make sure the cable can be tucked away and the unit is out of the way of children as the housing may become hot.

When you are deciding what to cook in your slow cooker, choose a recipe that will fit within the capacity of your cooker. Before you start your recipe, make sure that any dishes, bowls or pans you are using fit inside the cooker first. Imagine making a and finding the loaf pan does not fit in your slow cooker. If you intend to finish a dish under the grill/broiler, check the instruction manual first to see if you can put the cooking pot under a direct heat source.

How full should the pot be?

Liquids are the most important component when cooking in a slow cooker. There should always be liquid to start the cooking off with. Stews and casseroles generate liquid as they cook because of the water content of the food and the steaming that occurs during cooking time. This means that you could add only 100 ml/ ½ cup of water, stock or wine and find you have as much as 400 ml/2 cups at the end of the cooking time.

A joint of meat or chicken should not take up any more than three-quarters of the cooking pot, while a pan, baking dish or bowl should have an inch or so of space around it with the water coming roughly halfway up the side of the basin. When cooking soups, make sure that the liquid has a clearance of no less than 3 cm/1¼ inches from the top of the pot.

Do I need to preheat the slow cooker?

Refer to your manufacturer's instruction manual as some recommend a preheating time and others recommend switching the slow cooker to the desired setting only when it is filled with food.

Cooking times and heat settings

Timings and settings vary for the type of dish or cut of meat you are using, or how long you need your dish to cook for to fit in with your day: a slow cooker really can be used to suit your lifestyle and pace.

The LOW setting essentially suits smaller cuts of meat and dishes with ingredients that need gentle cooking. The low setting will eventually reach the same temperature as HIGH but just take a much longer time to do so.

LOW is good for:

- Diced meats, chicken joints, chops and cutlets
- Soups
- Bain marie method of cooking
- Fish or vegetable casseroles and curries

The HIGH setting can be used in a variety of ways, e.g. cooking large pieces of meat or if you want your dish to be cooked in a shorter time. As a rule, it will take half the time to cook a stew or casserole on HIGH than on the LOW setting. When thickening stews or casseroles, increase the temperature from LOW to HIGH, add your cornflour/ cornstarch, and cook for a further 20 minutes. HIGH is good for:

- Whole joints of meat or whole birds
- Steamed dishes or cakes and anything with a rising agent, such as dumplings
- Pâtés and terrines
- Soups

Some machines have an AUTO setting, which means the cooker starts off on HIGH then automatically turns itself down to LOW after a set time – this is great for giving your cooking an initial boost.

A WARM setting will keep your food hot if your mealtime is delayed, although it is not an essential setting. Keeping the cooker on LOW would not overcook your food, even if left for an extra few hours. The exception to this rule is if a dish contains pasta or rice.

Adjusting timings

If you want to speed up or slow down casseroles based on diced meat or vegetables so that the cooking fits around your schedule, adjust the heat settings and timings as below.

LOW	MEDIUM	HIGH
6–8 hours	4–6 hours	3–4 hours
8–10 hours	6–8 hours	5–6 hours
10–12 hours	8–10 hours	7–8 hours

TIP

Don't be tempted to lift the lid as this breaks the seal created by the steam between the lid and the cooking pot. Each time the lid is lifted, add an extra 20 minutes to the cooking time.

preparing food for the slow cooker

Good preparation of ingredients is key to using a slow cooker. Be well prepared and have everything ready the night before, if necessary.

Meat

Cheap cuts of meat are perfect for use in a slow cooker. For casseroles and stews, make sure the chunks of meat are cut to the same size. Forgotten cuts such as pig's cheeks or pork shanks are great for this method of cooking. Browning the meat will add flavour and colour to the finished dish but it is not imperative. For a healthier dish or if you are short on time, just add the meat raw. Whole birds or joints need to be cooked only on HIGH, but any other cut can be used on a setting to suit when you require it. Remove skin and fat from meats otherwise you may have a build up of liquid fat in your finished dishes.

Vegetables

Cut all vegetables the same size when preparing them for the slow cooker. Onions need softening in a little oil otherwise they tend to retain a bit of a bite, but other vegetables can go straight into the pot. Root vegetables can take longer to cook than the meat so make sure these are cut smaller than the chunks of meat for even and consistent cooking.

Fish

Fish responds really well in a slow cooker when cooked on LOW. The gentle cooking of this setting means the fish stays intact. Poach large fillets of fish or cook chunks of fish in a sauce. As shellfish only require a little cooking, add these for a short time at the end of cooking. Turn the slow cooker onto HIGH and cook for the last 15–20 minutes of the cooking time for your dish.

Pasta

Pasta will become unpleasantly stodgy, absorbing too much liquid if added at the beginning of the cooking time. Either cook in boiling water and stir through the finished dish to warm through or add for the last 30–40 minutes of cooking time only.

Rice

Rice can quickly become overcooked in a slow cooker as the grains split apart, but with a little experience it can be very easy to prepare well. Easy-cook rice is the best choice as it has been pre-washed and partially cooked by the manufacturer, giving you a less starchy finish. Basmati and long grain can work well too. Add rice to dishes 25–30 minutes from end of cooking time. The only exception here is rice puddings.

Pulses/Legumes

Dried pulses/legumes contain a toxin if not cooked properly so it is important to follow the correct method when using these in your slow cooker. Soak overnight then boil for at least 10 minutes before adding to the slow cooker. Exceptions to this rule are lentils and pearl barley which can be added directly.

TIP

Foods at the bottom of the cooking pot will cook faster so think about how you assemble your dish.

Cream and milk

Dishes such as rice pudding or custard will cook very well in your slow cooker but whole milk or cream will be less likely to split or curdle than skimmed dairy products due to the fat content. Always use whole milk and whipping or double/heavy cream. If you are making a creamy soup, always stir the cream through 15 minutes before the end of cooking time, not before.

TIP

Think about substituting canned pulses/legumes for dried. Slow cooking is all about economy and convenience, so the quicker the preparation, the more time you have to spend doing other things.

getting the most from your slow cooker

Your slow cooker is a very versatile piece of kitchen equipment that you will want to keep on using again and again. Don't just think about your slow cooker for making stews and casseroles. A slow cooker can also work like a conventional bain marie so it can be used for making baked custards and sweet or savoury dishes. The generous capacity of most models also makes it ideal for making large batches of chutneys and preserves. What about using it to make a rich, flavoursome chicken stock for use in soups?

Adapting your own recipes for a slow cooker

Adapting your own favourite recipes for a slow cooker is a simple process of comparison. Look for a similar recipe within this book which will give you an idea of how to prepare the ingredients and the approximate amounts you may need. Finding a similar recipe will also help you to determine the cooking time required. Reduce any liquids within your own recipe by at least half, making sure the ingredients are covered by about two thirds. Using fresh ingredients

TIP

Make sure that any stock or water you add to your recipe is hot to get the cooking temperature up to speed as soon as possible.

that contain lots of water (such as fresh tomatoes) will create liquid so you will need to add even less stock or water to the recipe to accommodate this.

Changing recipes to suit different models of slow cooker

If you need to adapt a recipe, it may be that you need to halve it for a small machine, or add half as much again to feed a larger crowd from a big slow cooker. The larger quantity may take a while longer to come up to heat. Therefore, if you are intending on cooking the recipe on LOW, start it off on HIGH for 30–60 minutes or set the cooker to AUTO to allow the food to reach the correct temperature more quickly. However, the actual cooking timings remain the same. If you are unsure of your slow cooker's capacity, measure with a jug/cups and water then you can roughly work out from the ingredient list the final quantity of your recipe.

Cooking for the freezer

Using a slow cooker is the perfect way to create 'convenience' food of your very own. Whether you live on your own or lead a busy family lifestyle, use your slow cooker to batch cook soups, casseroles, or stews. When cooling the food, it is important to do this as quickly as possible, so remove it from the slow cooker and transfer to freezerproof containers or freezer bags, uncovered or unsealed, then let cool. Cover, then freeze straight away. Defrost the portions in a fridge overnight or for about 4 hours at room temperature. Always reheat thoroughly until very hot before serving. You can do this in a pan on the hob/stovetop, or in a microwave. With a little forward planning you need never be without a good meal from your slow cooker.

TIP

If adding wine to a recipe, especially red, reduce it in a saucepan set over the hob/stovetop by at least a quarter to cook out the alcohol before adding to the slow cooker. The temperature within the slow cooker is not hot enough to do this and can result in a bitter-tasting dish.

soups, appetizers & light bites

slow-cooked onion and cider soup with Gruyère toasts

50 g/3 tablespoons butter

1 kg/2¼ lbs. onions, sliced

4 garlic cloves, crushed

1 litre/4 cups vegetable stock

375 ml/1½ cups sweet/hard cider

2 egg yolks

CHEESE TOASTS (OPTIONAL):

4 thin slices of baguette or similar

100 g/4 oz. Gruyère cheese, thinly sliced

SERVES 4

Onions are so versatile to cook with. The delicious soup is comforting and filling, especially with the addition of the cheesy toasts floating on top, but these are optional.

Put the butter in a saucepan set over medium heat. Add the onions and garlic, partially cover with a lid and cook for about 20 minutes, stirring often so that the onions become silky soft without burning. Transfer to the slow cooker, add the stock and cider and cover with the lid. Cook on HIGH for about 3 hours or until the onions are tender and the soup is thick and golden. Remove from the heat and slowly whisk in the egg yolks. Cover and keep warm.

Preheat the grill/broiler. Toast the bread under the hot grill/broiler until lightly golden on one side only. Put the Gruyère slices on the untoasted side and cook under the grill/broiler until the cheese is golden brown and bubbling. Ladle the soup into warmed serving bowls and sit a Gruyère toast on top of each to serve.

Italian pasta and bean soup

2 tablespoons olive oil

1 large onion, finely chopped

2 garlic cloves, finely chopped

1 large potato, peeled and diced

4 ripe tomatoes, coarsely chopped

1 tablespoon tomato purée/paste

1.25 litres/5 cups chicken or vegetable stock

a sprig of fresh thyme, sage, or rosemary

2 x 400-g/14-oz. cans cannellini beans, drained and rinsed

150 g/5 oz. small dried pasta shapes, such as orecchiette

a pinch of dried red chilli/hot pepper flakes

salt and freshly ground black pepper

freshly grated Parmesan cheese, to serve

SERVES 4

This hearty soup of pasta and beans is a classic from the region of Puglia in Italy. The pasta shapes traditionally used are orecchiette, meaning "little ears," but you can use any shape you have to hand.

Heat the oil in a large saucepan, add the onion, garlic and potato, and cook for 3–4 minutes until golden. Add the tomatoes, tomato purée/paste, stock, herbs and beans. Season to taste then transfer to a slow cooker, cover and cook on HIGH for 3½ hours.

Remove the lid, add the pasta and chilli/pepper flakes and stir. Cook for a further 20–30 minutes depending upon what pasta shapes you use, or until the pasta is al dente. Ladle into bowls and serve sprinkled with a little Parmesan.

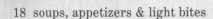

Spanish chickpea soup with chorizo, paprika and saffron

2 tablespoons extra virgin olive oil

1 onion, chopped

3 thin celery stalks, chopped, with leaves reserved

1 large carrot, chopped

2 garlic cloves, chopped

225 g/8 oz. chorizo, skinned, halved, then cut into 1-cm/½-inch slices

400-g/14-oz. can chickpeas, drained and rinsed

1.75 litres/7 cups chicken stock

¼ teaspoon Spanish smoked hot paprika (pimentón picante) or ½ teaspoon paprika

125 g/4 oz. fresh spinach, tough stalks removed and leaves coarsely chopped into large pieces

¼ teaspoon saffron threads, bruised with a mortar and pestle

Manchego or Parmesan cheese, shaved, to serve (optional)

SERVES 4

This hearty soup is a meal in itself. Chunks of chorizo or other sausage float alongside chickpeas and spinach in a slightly smoky, fragrant broth. The special flavour comes from two typically Spanish spices, pimentón and its home-grown luxury spice, saffron.

Heat the oil in a large saucepan and add the chopped onion, celery, and carrot. Gently sauté the vegetables for 5 minutes, until they begin to soften. Add the garlic, chorizo, chickpeas, stock and pimentón. Bring to the boil then transfer to the slow cooker. Cook on HIGH for 2 hours.

Add the spinach and reserved celery leaves and cook for a further 15 minutes. Add the saffron. Clean out the mortar with a little stock and add that too. Cook for a further 15 minutes.

Serve hot in large, wide bowls. Add shavings of cheese, if using, and serve with plenty of bread.

1 tablespoon olive oil

1 red onion, chopped

2 garlic cloves, crushed

2 leeks, well cleaned and sliced

2 carrots, diced

2 celery stalks, diced

4 thick slices of bacon, diced

400-g/14-oz. can haricot/navy or cannellini beans, drained and rinsed

1.2 litres/5 cups chicken or vegetable stock

1½ tablespoons tomato purée/paste

1 dried bay leaf

a small bunch of fresh thyme

75 g/½ cup tiny pasta shapes

fresh pesto or freshly grated Parmesan, to serve (optional)

SERVES 4

This classic Italian soup is always popular and is the perfect recipe for cooking in a slow cooker. Serve with a swirl of fresh pesto or freshly grated Parmesan.

classic minestrone

Heat the oil in a saucepan, add the onion, garlic, leeks, carrots, celery and bacon, and sauté for 10 minutes over medium heat without browning. Add the beans, stock, tomato purée/paste and herbs, bring to the boil and transfer to the slow cooker.

Cover with the lid and cook on HIGH for 2 hours. Add the pasta shapes, replace the lid and cook for a further 30 minutes.

Season and serve with a spoonful of pesto, if using, and plenty of crusty bread.

chicken soup

1 tablespoon olive oil

1 onion, chopped

1 garlic clove, crushed

2 chicken breasts, diced

2 leeks, well cleaned and chopped

200 g/7 oz. potatoes, unpeeled and chopped

1 litre/4 cups hot chicken stock

3 sprigs of fresh thyme

2 dried bay leaves

200-g can/1 cup sweetcorn/corn kernels, drained

sea salt and freshly ground black pepper

SERVES 4

A bowlful of this traditional comforting soup makes everyone feel better, especially when served with plenty of warmed bread.

Heat the olive oil in a saucepan, add the onion, garlic, chicken and leeks, and sauté gently for 8 minutes without browning. Add the potatoes, hot stock, thyme and bay leaves, then season lightly.

Transfer the ingredients to the slow cooker, cover with the lid and cook on HIGH for 4 hours. About 1 hour before serving, stir in the (sweet) corn. Remove the thyme and bay leaves and check the seasoning before serving.

Squash is a wonderfully versatile and delicious vegetable, and it's used to great effect in this flavourful soup.

golden butternut squash soup

1-kg/2-lb. butternut squash, peeled

2 tablespoons olive oil

2 onions, diced

1 garlic clove, crushed

1.2 litres/5 cups chicken or vegetable stock

sea salt and freshly ground black pepper

single/light cream, to serve (optional)

SERVES 4

Cut the squash in half lengthwise and use a spoon to scoop out the seeds. Chop the squash into 2-cm/1-inch pieces.

Heat the oil in a large saucepan, add the onions and garlic and sauté over low heat for 10 minutes. Add the chopped squash pieces and the stock and bring to the boil.

Transfer to the slow cooker, cover with the lid, and cook on HIGH for 1 hour.

Using a hand-held blender or liquidizer, blitz the soup until smooth and creamy. Season to taste and serve with a swirl of cream, if liked.

garlic and chilli/chile rice soup with wilted greens

2 tablespoons vegetable oil

4 teaspoons sesame oil

4 garlic cloves, chopped

8 spring onions/scallions, finely chopped

4 teaspoons finely grated fresh ginger

2 small red fresh chillies/chiles, seeded and thinly sliced

200 g/½ cup long grain white rice

1.5 litres/6 cups vegetable stock

2 tablespoons soy sauce or Thai fish sauce

a bunch of spring/collard greens, roughly shredded

a small bunch of fresh coriander/cilantro, chopped

ground white pepper

SERVES 4

This is a substantial soup — really more of a light stew. Boiled rice soups are popular in many Asian countries, especially China. Instead of the spring/collard greens, you can use the fresh, young outer leaves of any brassicas such as cabbage. They work very nicely with the simple Asian flavours here.

Put the oils in a saucepan and set over high heat. Add the garlic and spring onions/scallions and cook until the garlic is turning golden (burnt garlic is very bitter and not nice at all). This will give the soup a lovely, nutty garlic flavour. Add the ginger, chillies/chiles and rice to the pan and stir-fry in the garlic-infused oil for 1 minute. Add the stock and soy sauce and bring to the boil.

Transfer to the slow cooker, cover with the lid, and cook on HIGH for 1½ hours. Add the chopped greens and cook for a further 30 minutes, until they turn emerald green and are tender. Ladle the soup into warmed serving bowls, sprinkle the coriander/cilantro over the top and season to taste with pepper.

Scotch broth

2 tablespoons light olive oil

2 carrots, diced

1 leek, well cleaned and diced

2 celery stalks, diced and leaves chopped

500 g/1 lb. stewing lamb, well trimmed of fat and diced into small cubes

1 litre/4 cups hot chicken stock

1 tablespoon light soy sauce

95 g/½ cup brown rice

sea salt and freshly ground black pepper

soft white/dinner rolls, buttered, to serve

SERVES 4

From the land that brings us haggis, kippers, neeps and tatties comes its famous namesake broth. Barley is traditionally used but this recipe features wholesome brown rice — use whichever you prefer.

Heat the oil in a large saucepan. Add the carrots, leek, celery and celery leaves and cook over high heat for 5 minutes, stirring often. Add the lamb and cook for a further 5 minutes, until the meat is browned.

Transfer the vegetables and lamb to the slow cooker. Add the hot chicken stock and soy sauce. Cover with the lid and cook on HIGH for 2 hours, until the vegetables are cooked. Add the brown rice, replace the lid and cook for 1 hour further.

Season to taste and serve with soft, buttered rolls.

This classic soup is based on a French recipe for Grape Harvester Soup, traditionally served to hungry grape-pickers. The original would have used much more garlic — perhaps as much as four heads of garlic rather than a mere four cloves. When garlic is cooked very slowly and for a long time, it loses much of its pungency and the flavour becomes mellow and nutty.

fresh tomato and garlic soup

3 tablespoons olive oil

500 g/1 lb. onions, thinly sliced

4 garlic cloves, finely chopped

450 g/1 lb. ripe plum tomatoes, skinned, seeded, and chopped

½ teaspoon sugar

1 litre/4 cups vegetable stock

150 ml/⅔ cup white wine

sea salt

4 slices of stale bread, to serve

SERVES 4

Heat the oil in a saucepan, add the onions and gently sauté for 10 minutes until golden and very soft. Add to the slow cooker with the garlic, tomatoes, sugar, stock and wine. Season with salt. Cover with the lid and cook on HIGH for 4 hours.

To serve, place the slices of bread in the base of heated soup plates and spoon the soup over the top.

slow cooker stock

2 carcasses uncooked chicken,
1 kg/2 lbs. wings, or 1 turkey
drumstick, sliced

any giblets or trimmings such as
wingtips from the chickens

4 carrots, sliced

1 leek, well cleaned and sliced

1 onion, sliced or chopped

1 celery stalk

1 teaspoon black peppercorns

1 fresh bay leaf

1 sprig of fresh thyme

2–3 fresh parsley stalks

2 tablespoons white wine or
1 tablespoon white wine vinegar

MAKES ABOUT 2 QUARTS

A slow cooker is a convenient way to make an all-purpose fresh chicken stock, which can be frozen and stored for use in a wide variety of recipes, such as soups and casseroles.

Put all the ingredients in the slow cooker, cover with cold water and cook on LOW for at least 12 hours or overnight. Strain, leave to cool and freeze in smaller portions for convenience.

125 ml/½ cup sweet white wine such as German Riesling or Gewürztraminer

400 g/14 oz. creamy blue cheese, such as Gorgonzola or Roquefort, coarsely chopped

1 teaspoon cornflour/cornstarch mixed with 1 tablespoon of the wine

TO SERVE:

4–6 ripe pears, quartered, or 24 asparagus spears, lightly cooked

grissini (breadsticks)

SERVES 6

blue cheese fondue

Blue cheese, fresh walnuts and juicy pears make a delicious combination. This fondue is perfect served as an appetizer with asparagus tips for dipping, or as a dessert with pears.

To prepare the fondue, pour the wine into the slow cooker and heat on HIGH until warm — this may take 30 minutes. Switch to LOW and gradually stir in the blue cheese followed by the cornflour/cornstarch mixture, stirring constantly for about 45 minutes, until the cheese has melted and the mixture is smooth. Serve with grissini and pears or asparagus for dipping, as preferred.

vacherin fondue with caramelized shallots

30 g/2 tablespoons unsalted butter

300 g/10 oz. shallots, thinly sliced

2 teaspoons light brown sugar

250 ml/1 cup dry white wine

300 g/10 oz. Gruyère cheese, grated

1 tablespoon plain/all-purpose flour

10 oz. Vacherin, Fontina or raclette cheese, grated

TO SERVE:

baguette, sliced

cherry tomatoes

SERVES 6

Vacherin is a wonderfully flavourful cheese. It is not as sweet as Emmental, and so is perfect here with the sweetness of caramelized shallots. Substitute Fontina or raclette if it is unavailable.

Melt the butter in a sauté pan set over medium heat. Add the shallots, reduce the heat to low and gently cook for 30 minutes until the shallots are caramelized. Arrange them in the base of the slow cooker dish. Stir in the sugar, wine, Gruyère, flour and Vacherin.

Cover and cook on LOW for 2 hours, stirring occasionally, until the cheese has melted.

Serve the fondue with cubes of bread and cherry tomatoes for dipping. Alternatively, put slices of baguette into individual serving bowls and ladle the fondue over the top.

Tip

To peel the shallots, place them in a bowl and cover them with boiling water. Leave them for 1 minute, then drain. When the shallots are cool enough to handle, top and tail them with a knife and the skin will peel easily away.

This is a chunky terrine of pork, flavoured with fennel seeds and layered with spinach. Its small size makes it perfect for a small party of guests or to serve for a simple snack or lunch.

pork, fennel, and spinach terrine

2 fresh bay leaves

150 g/5 oz. dry-cured streaky bacon

100 g/2 cups fresh spinach, chopped

2 tablespoons olive oil

1 small onion, chopped

1 teaspoon fennel seeds, crushed

2 garlic cloves, finely chopped

300 g/10 oz. pork belly, coarsely minced/ground pork

200 g/7 oz. lean pork fillet/pork tenderloin, diced

½ teaspoon ground nutmeg

½ teaspoon ground allspice

1 teaspoon sea salt

½ teaspoon black pepper

crusty bread, to serve

a loaf pan or terrine mould, about 850-ml/3-cup capacity, lightly oiled

SERVES 6

Arrange the bay leaves over the bottom of the loaf pan, then lay enough bacon across the width to cover the base, reserving any slices left, to cover the top of the terrine later. Put the spinach in a colander and pour over boiling water to blanch. Refresh with cold water, squeeze out any excess water and set aside.

Heat the olive oil in a frying pan/skillet over low heat and sauté the onion, fennel seeds and garlic for 3–5 minutes, or until soft but not yet brown. Transfer to a large bowl with half of the spinach, the minced/ground pork and fillet/tenderloin, nutmeg and allspice. Add the salt and pepper and mix well.

Put half of the pork mixture in the prepared loaf pan and press down firmly. Top with the remaining spinach, then the remaining pork mixture. Press down firmly, then fold over any overhanging bacon and use the reserved slices to cover the top of the terrine. Tightly cover with oiled foil and sit in the slow cooker. Fill the slow cooker with enough water to come halfway up the sides of the terrine. Cover the slow cooker with the lid and cook on HIGH for 4 hours.

Transfer to a dish to catch any juices and put a weight on top. Let cool, then chill overnight or for 1–2 days. Serve with crusty bread.

smoked and fresh salmon terrine

250 g/8 oz. skinless salmon fillet, cut into chunks

1 teaspoon finely grated orange zest/peel

2 teaspoons fresh orange juice

4 tablespoons/¼ cup chopped fresh dill

350 g/12 oz. smoked salmon

2 egg whites, chilled and lightly whisked

150 ml/⅔ cup whipping/heavy cream, chilled

freshly ground white pepper

baby salad leaves/greens, to serve

HAZELNUT DRESSING:

3 tablespoons olive oil

1 tablespoon hazelnut oil

½ tablespoon freshly squeezed lemon juice

2 tablespoons chopped hazelnuts

2 tablespoons chopped fresh parsley

sea salt and freshly ground black pepper

a loaf pan or terrine mould, about 850-ml/3-cup capacity, lightly oiled and base-lined with baking parchment

SERVES 6

A mousseline is a mousse of fish, shellfish or poultry lightened with cream and egg whites. When made with salmon, it is the most beautiful elegant golden-pink. It is amazingly easy to prepare in a slow cooker too, with a spectacular effect that makes a very luxurious appetizer or posh picnic dish.

Put the chunks of fresh salmon into a food processor with the orange zest/peel, orange juice, dill and plenty of pepper. Blend until smooth. Remove the bowl from the food processor, cover and chill.

Meanwhile, roughly chop half the smoked salmon. Put the bowl back on the processor. With the machine running, add the egg whites through the tube, then the cream. Blend until thick and smooth — do not overwork or it will curdle. Scrape into a bowl and stir in the chopped smoked salmon.

Carefully fill the prepared loaf pan with the mixture, packing it down well. Level the surface and cover the top with buttered baking parchment. Stand in the slow cooker and pour in enough hot water to come halfway up the sides. Cover with the lid and cook on HIGH for 2 hours, until firm.

Remove from the slow cooker, let cool completely, then chill in the refrigerator. Loosen the edges with a thin knife and turn out onto a board. Trim and tidy up the edges and pat dry. Wrap the terrine with the remaining smoked salmon, pressing down well, then transfer to a flat serving platter.

Put the salad in a small bowl; whisk the dressing ingredients together, then pour over the leaves/greens and toss gently. Slice the terrine with a very sharp knife and serve with the salad.

This pâté is great party fare. It was inspired by 'tinga', a dish of Mexican shredded beef, and relies on slow cooking and a few key flavours. Even though it calls for a cheap cut of beef, it pays to use the best quality you can find.

beef and ale pâté

2 tablespoons olive oil

5 large, mild fresh red chillies/chiles

3 whole garlic cloves, peeled

600 g/1¼ lbs. chuck/blade steak, trimmed of fat and cut into 2-cm/1-inch chunks

2 x 330-ml/12-oz. bottles of ale

400-g/14-oz. can pinto beans, drained

sea salt

8 tablespoons/½ cup chopped fresh coriander/cilantro, to garnish

tortilla chips, to serve

MAKES ABOUT 750 ML/3 CUPS

Heat the olive oil in a large, heavy-based saucepan set over medium/low heat. Cut the green stalk ends from 3 of the red chillies/chiles. Put these chillies/chiles and the garlic in the saucepan and gently cook for 3 minutes. Increase the heat to medium/high, add the steak, and cook, stirring occasionally, for 5 minutes until the meat is browned.

Add the ale to the saucepan and bring to the boil. Transfer the ingredients to the slow cooker and cover with the lid. Cook for 7 hours on HIGH. About 2 hours before the end of cooking time, add the canned beans and stir well. The meat should be falling apart at the end of the cooking time.

Put the meat with its accompanying ingredients and a little of the cooking liquid in a food processor and process briefly until you have a coarse pâté. Season to taste with salt. Spoon into a serving dish. Cut the remaining red chillies/chiles into thin strips and scatter over the pâté along with the coriander/cilantro. Serve warm or at room temperature with tortilla chips for dipping.

These are like little savoury cheesecakes, served warm with a drizzle of olive oil or a small spoonful of rich tomato sauce. Straining the ricotta makes the mixture lighter so is worth the additional effort. Beat the eggs into the cheese very well for even more lightness, and be careful with the seasoning — the capers and olives are both quite salty already.

spinach and ricotta timbales

10 sun-dried (or sun-blushed) tomatoes in oil, drained

250 g/8 oz. fresh spinach

500 g/1 lb. ricotta, well drained

3 large eggs, beaten

12 small Greek-style black olives, pitted and coarsely chopped

2 tablespoons chopped fresh basil or oregano

2 tablespoons salted capers, rinsed and chopped, plus extra whole capers to serve

freshly grated nutmeg

sea salt and freshly ground black pepper

olive oil or fresh tomato sauce, to serve

6 dariole moulds or 125-ml/¹/₂-cup capacity ramekins, well buttered

SERVES 6

Put a sun-dried tomato in the bottom of each mould or ramekin. Thinly slice the remaining sun-dried tomatoes.

To prepare the spinach, remove the tough stems from the leaves, then wash the leaves really well and put in a saucepan while still wet. Cook until the leaves wilt, then plunge into cold water. Drain very well and squeeze to extract any excess moisture. Loosen the leaves slightly.

Push the ricotta through a fine-mesh sieve to make it fluffy, then beat in the eggs. Lightly stir in the drained, wilted spinach, sliced sun-dried tomatoes, olives, basil or oregano, and capers. Taste and season lightly with salt, pepper, and nutmeg.

Spoon the ricotta mixture into the moulds and level, then put them in the slow cooker. Carefully fill the slow cooker with boiling water to come halfway up the moulds. Cover and cook on HIGH for 50 minutes, until almost set and a little puffed. Remove from the slow cooker and let cool slightly. Turn out onto small plates, then serve at room temperature with extra capers and a sprinkle of olive oil or a spoonful of fresh tomato sauce.

eggs cocotte

60 g/2 oz. fresh spinach, chopped

4 large eggs

4 tablespoons milk

75 g/¾ cup grated Parmesan cheese

sea salt and freshly ground
black pepper

hot buttered toast, to serve

4 ovenproof ramekins, buttered

SERVES 4

*These baked eggs go down a treat at breakfast,
brunch or as a light dinner. If you can't fit four
ramekins in your slow cooker you could try placing
one on top of the others as it should still cook well.*

Divide the spinach between the prepared ramekins. Crack an
egg on top, add a spoonful of milk to each, then season and top
with the grated Parmesan. Place in the slow cooker and pour
in enough boiling water to come halfway up the dishes. Cover
with the lid and cook for 35–40 minutes on HIGH, until the
eggs have set. Serve with hot buttered toast.

meat
dishes

Yankee pot roast

3 tablespoons oil or bacon fat

1 tablespoon ground allspice

1 teaspoon sea salt

2 tablespoons plain/all-purpose flour

1 tablespoon dry mustard

1 kg/2 lbs. rolled silverside/boneless beef chuck

150 ml/⅔ red wine

100 ml/⅓ cup beef stock

4 parsnips, cut into 5-cm/ 2-inch chunks

2 sweet potatoes, cut into 5-cm/ 2-inch chunks

2 carrots, cut into 5-cm/2-inch chunks

12 small red onions, cut into 4 wedges through the root

2 tablespoons cornflour/cornstarch

sea salt and freshly ground black pepper

creamy mashed potatoes, to serve

SERVES 4

The pot roast is one of the great American classics and when it appears with braised vegetables, it becomes Yankee Pot Roast. Serve with a big mound of creamy mashed potatoes.

Put 1 tablespoon of the oil, the allspice, salt, flour and mustard in a small bowl and mix to form a paste, adding more oil as necessary. Rub the beef with the mixture, cover and marinate in the fridge for 3 hours or overnight.

Remove the meat and shake off any excess spices. Heat the remaining oil or bacon fat in a large frying pan/skillet, add the meat and brown on all sides. Transfer to the slow cooker.

Add the wine to the frying pan/skillet, bring to the boil and cook until reduced by two-thirds. Pour over the meat along with the stock, cover with the lid and cook on HIGH for 7 hours. Add the vegetables and cook for 1 further hour. Mix the cornflour/ cornstarch with 3 tablespoons water and blend it into the gravy. Cook for a further 15 minutes then serve with some creamy mashed potatoes.

2 tablespoons olive oil

2 onions, diced

3 garlic cloves, crushed

700 g/1½ lbs. lean minced/ground beef

2 tablespoons tomato purée/paste

600 ml/2⅓ cups passata (Italian strained tomatoes)

1 tablespoon cayenne pepper

1 tablespoon Spanish smoked sweet paprika (pimentón dulce)

2 x 400-g/14-oz. cans red kidney beans, drained and rinsed

sea salt and freshly ground black pepper

TO SERVE:

3 tablespoons of fresh coriander/cilantro leaves, chopped

boiled white rice

guacamole (optional)

SERVES 4–6

chili con carne

Long, slow cooking is the secret of good chili. Simple dishes are often the best, and they don't come much simpler than this. You can add more or less cayenne pepper, depending on how hot you like your food.

Heat the oil in a large saucepan, add the onions and garlic and sauté gently for 5 minutes. Add the beef, breaking it up with a wooden spoon, and cook for a further 5 minutes or until browned. Add the beef mixture to the slow cooker and stir in the tomato purée/paste, passata, cayenne pepper and paprika and season well.

Cover with the lid and cook on HIGH for 5 hours, adding the kidney beans 1 hour before the end of cooking time just to warm them through.

Just before serving, stir in the chopped coriander/cilantro and serve with rice and a bowl of guacamole, if liked.

chunky diner-style chili

1 kg/2¼ lbs. braising steak, cut into 4-cm/1½-inch chunks

500 ml/2 cups beer

2 tablespoons olive oil

2 large onions, roughly chopped

6 garlic cloves, finely chopped

1 fresh red chilli/chile, seeded and finely chopped

2 x 400-g/14-oz. cans chopped tomatoes

3 tablespoons cider vinegar

1 tablespoon brown sugar

1 tablespoon Spanish smoked sweet paprika (pimentón dulce)

1 tablespoon mild chilli powder

2 tablespoons ground cumin

400-g/14-oz. can kidney, borlotti or pinto beans, drained and rinsed

sea salt and freshly ground pepper

TO SERVE:

boiled white rice

chopped red onion

a handful of fresh coriander/cilantro leaves, chopped

crackers (optional)

SERVES 4–6

A chunky chili con carne is a diner institution, traditionally served with little cellophane packages of saltine crackers. Chunks of tender steak and puréed dried chillies/chiles make this mouth-watering version a bit more special.

Put the beef in a bowl, pour the beer over and let marinate for 30 minutes. Drain, reserving 150 ml/⅔ cup of the liquid and pat the beef dry with paper towels.

In a large saucepan, heat 1 tablespoon of the olive oil. Season the meat and sear in batches until evenly browned. Remove from the pan and set aside. Add the remaining olive oil and sauté the onions, garlic and chilli/chile for 5 minutes. Put the meat and onion mixture into the slow cooker.

Add the chopped tomatoes, cider vinegar, brown sugar, paprika, chilli powder and cumin and season well. Cover with the lid and cook on HIGH for 6 hours, adding the beans 1 hour before the end of cooking time just to warm them through.

Serve in small bowls with your choice of accompaniments: cooked rice, chopped red onion, coriander/cilantro or crackers, if liked.

Here, a classic meatloaf is served with a spicy tomato sauce. All it needs is a side of green beans to make a satisfying family meal.

meatloaf with tomato sauce

12 slices of Parma ham or prosciutto

200 g/7 oz. chicken livers, chopped

400 g/14 oz. lean pork, diced

300 g/10 oz. minced/ground turkey or chicken

1 red onion, diced

2 eggs, beaten

3 fresh bay leaves, torn

a bunch of fresh flat leaf parsley, chopped

sea salt and freshly ground black pepper

TOMATO SAUCE:

3 tablespoons olive oil

1 onion, diced

2 garlic cloves, crushed

2 x 400-g/14-oz. cans chopped tomatoes

a 1-kg/2-lb. loaf pan

SERVES 6

Line the loaf pan with the Parma ham, leaving some aside to cover the top of the finished meatloaf.

Put the chicken livers in a bowl with the pork and turkey, add the onion, eggs, bay leaves and parsley, season and mix well. This is best done with your hands.

Fill the prepared pan with the meat, level the top and cover with the remaining ham. Cover with foil and place in the slow cooker. Carefully pour enough boiling water to come halfway up the sides of the pan and cook on HIGH for 4 hours. Remove and let stand for 10 minutes. Drain off any juice into a jug/pitcher, then turn out the meatloaf onto a deep plate.

To make the tomato sauce, heat the oil and sauté the onion gently for 5 minutes in a saucepan. Add the garlic and cook for a further 5 minutes. Add the tomatoes and reserved meat juices, season and simmer gently for 30 minutes, stirring frequently. Serve the sauce alongside slices of the meatloaf.

Notes: If you prefer your meatloaf a bit browner, place it in an oven preheated to 200°C (400°F) Gas 6 for 10 minutes to brown before serving. If your slow cooker cannot take a 1-kg/2-lb. pan, divide the mixture into two portions and cook one portion in a 500-g/1-lb. loaf pan, adjusting the cooking time to 3 hours. Freeze the second portion and cook another time.

Provençal daube of beef

4 tablespoons olive oil

500 g/1 lb. onions, sliced

2 garlic cloves, sliced

2 tomatoes, chopped

1 carrot, sliced crossways

2 sprigs of fresh thyme

2 fresh bay leaves

1 kg/2 lbs. rolled rib of beef/
boneless beef rib-eye, in one piece

100 ml/⅓ cup white wine

6 green olives, pitted

6 black olives, pitted

sea salt and freshly ground
black pepper

TO SERVE:

creamy mashed potatoes

steamed baby carrots

SERVES 4

Daubes are dishes in which the meat is simmered in wine for a long time and is so soft that it can be cut with a spoon. The wine used here is a white one, which is rather unexpected with beef. It gives a more acid pungency to the dish and goes well with the traditional olives.

Heat 2 tablespoons of the oil in a large frying pan/skillet. Add the onions and sauté until softened but not browned. Add the garlic, tomatoes, carrot, thyme and bay leaves and sauté until lightly browned. Transfer to the slow cooker. Add the remaining oil and beef to the frying pan/skillet, brown it on all sides then transfer to the slow cooker.

Pour the wine into the frying pan/skillet, scraping any brown bits into the liquid. Season with salt and pepper and pour this mixture over the beef. Cover with the lid and cook on LOW for 8–10 hours. Add the olives to the casserole for the last 30 minutes of cooking time just to heat through.

Serve with lots of creamy mashed potatoes and a few steamed baby carrots — the beef should be so tender that it falls to pieces when touched.

Irish carbonnade

750 g/1½ lbs. skirt/flank steak, cut into 1½-inch cubes

3 tablespoons soft brown sugar

1 onion, chopped

4 tablespoons plain/all-purpose flour

12 shallots, peeled (see Tip on page 38)

500 ml/2 cups beef stock

375 ml/1½ cups dark Irish stout, such as Guinness

2 tablespoons red wine vinegar

3 cloves

1 fresh or 2 dried bay leaves

sea salt and freshly ground black pepper

IRISH CHEDDAR CROÛTES:

12 slices of baguette

olive oil, for drizzling

150 g/6 oz. strong/sharp Cheddar cheese (preferably Irish), grated

SERVES 4

Carbonnades are native to Belgium and northern France, where they are always flavoured with beer, but a good Irish stout actually gives an even tastier result. Lots of sweet shallots or pickling onions add a little sweetness and balance the flavours nicely.

Put all the carbonnade ingredients in the slow cooker and mix well. Cover with the lid and cook on HIGH for 6–7 hours, until the meat is tender.

To make the Irish Cheddar croûtes, preheat the oven to 200°C (400°F) Gas 6. Arrange the baguette slices on a baking sheet and drizzle both sides with olive oil. Toast in the preheated oven for about 5 minutes, until golden brown. Remove from the oven, pile each croûte with grated cheese, and return to the oven to cook until the cheese has melted. Serve hot with the carbonnade.

steak and kidney pudding

2 tablespoons plain/all-purpose flour

½ teaspoon salt

¼ teaspoon freshly ground
black pepper

500 g/1 lb. braising steak, cut into
3-cm/1½-inch cubes

250 g/9 oz. beef kidney, cut into 2-cm/
1-inch chunks and membrane
discarded

1 large onion, chopped

1 garlic clove, crushed

300 ml/1¼ cups beef stock

SUET CRUST:

250 g/2 cups self-raising/rising flour

½ teaspoon salt

125 g/4½ oz. suet or shortening

*a 1-litre/1-quart ceramic bowl,
lightly greased*

SERVES 4

*The richness of the gravy in this traditional British
recipe is produced by the meats giving up their tasty
juices to thicken and flavour the stock.*

To make the suet crust, put the flour, salt and suet into a bowl and
add about 150 ml/ ⅔ cup water. Mix to form a ball. Reserve one-
third of the dough to make the lid and transfer the remainder to
a floured surface. Roll out to a circle large enough to line the
ceramic bowl. Use to line the bowl, cutting out a wedge to help
the fit and letting it overlap the edges by 2 cm/¾ inch all round.
Trim the excess and stick any joins together with a little water.

Put the flour, salt and pepper into a plastic bag, seal and shake.
Add the steak and kidney and shake vigorously until all the meat
is evenly coated with the seasoned flour. Shake off any excess
flour and transfer the meat to the prepared bowl, layering with
the onion and garlic as you do so.

Heat the stock, season to taste, then pour about half of it over the
meat to cover. Reserve the remaining stock (this can be served as
a sauce with second helpings).

Roll out the remaining dough to make a circle just big enough
to cover the top of the bowl. Fold the overlapping edges of the
pastry inwards over the top of the meat and brush the top edge
with water. Put the lid of pastry on top of the bowl and crimp the
edges inside the rim to seal the pudding.

Fold a sheet of foil down the middle to make a pleat — this will
allow for expansion. Put on top of the bowl and tie a length of
kitchen twine firmly around the edge, under the lip of the bowl.
Tie a handle of twine from side to side. Use this handle to lower
the pudding into the slow cooker. Three-quarters fill the cooker
with boiling water and cover with the lid. Cook on HIGH for
6 hours, not lifting the lid. Serve with the reserved stock.

navarin of lamb

1 kg/2 lbs. boneless shoulder of lamb

2 tablespoons olive oil

1 tablespoon sugar

2 tablespoons plain/all-purpose flour

500 ml/2 cups lamb or beef stock

200-g/7-oz. can Italian plum
tomatoes

2 garlic cloves, crushed

1 teaspoon chopped fresh
thyme leaves

1 sprig of fresh rosemary

1 dried bay leaf

12 new potatoes, scraped and cooked

12 baby carrots, scraped and cooked

125 g/1 cup peas, cooked

125 g/1 cup green beans, cooked and
cut into 1-cm/½-inch strips

sea salt and freshly ground
black pepper

SERVES 4–6

To give the sauce its rich colour and sweet flavour, a little sugar is sprinkled either onto the lamb as it is browned, or into the pan, which makes it easier to control. It is then caramelized: the darker the sugar becomes, the less sweet the stew will be.

Cut the lamb into 2-cm1-inch cubes, discarding any fat. Heat the oil in a heavy frying pan/skillet. Season the lamb and sauté in 2 batches, browning the pieces evenly all over and draining them of fat as they are put aside onto a dish.

Reserve 3 tablespoons of the fat in the pan. Sprinkle the sugar into the pan and let caramelize to a deep golden brown. (Take care not to caramelize it too much — it burns easily.) Quickly mix in the flour, then return the meat to the pan and mix well: this will let the flour cook a little.

Add the stock, tomatoes, garlic and herbs. Stir gently and bring to the boil. Season to taste, then transfer to the slow cooker. Cover with the lid and cook on HIGH for 4½ hours.

Taste and adjust the seasoning, then add the cooked vegetables. Mix them gently through the liquid and cook on HIGH for 1 further hour before serving.

This is a very simple dish but surprisingly effective considering how few ingredients there are, so make sure you adjust the seasoning carefully as it makes such a difference. Ideally, each steak should be about 2 cm/1 inch thick and weigh about 250 g/9 oz. Trim the stem end only of the okra, taking off the tiniest layer of the already-cut surface, to discourage the sticky liquid from oozing out.

Greek braised lamb with okra

3 tablespoons olive oil

4 lamb steaks, about 1 kg/2 lbs., cut from the leg and deboned

1 small onion, sliced

2 garlic cloves, crushed

4 tomatoes, skinned, seeded, and chopped

175 g/6 oz. okra, trimmed

sea salt and freshly ground black pepper

boiled new potatoes, to serve

chopped fresh flat-leaf parsley

SERVES 4

Heat the oil in a large saucepan. Season the meat with salt and pepper, add to the saucepan and brown the pieces all over. Use a slotted spoon to transfer the browned meat to the slow cooker.

Add the onion and garlic to the saucepan and cook until softened and lightly browned. Add the tomatoes and simmer until they are soft and pulpy. Add the tomato mixture to the lamb steaks in the slow cooker, turning the lamb steaks over to ensure the meat is well coated.

Cover with the lid and cook on HIGH for 3 hours. After 2 hours, add the prepared okra, tucking the fingers under the lamb steaks so that they are coated with sauce. Cook for 1 further hour, check the seasoning and adjust if necessary. Serve with new potatoes sprinkled with the chopped parsley.

4 tablespoons olive oil

350 g/12 oz. carrots, cut into 3-cm/
1-inch chunks

4 onions, peeled but left whole

4 small turnips, peeled but left whole

1 sprig of fresh thyme

1 dried or fresh bay leaf

6 peppercorns

6 garlic cloves, or to taste, crushed

2-kg/4-lbs. hand of pork (picnic
shoulder), rind removed

250 g/9 oz. smoked streaky bacon in
the piece, cut into chunks

400-g/14-oz. can cannellini beans,
drained and rinsed

750 g/1 lb. new potatoes, peeled

250 g/9 oz. green beans

sea salt and freshly ground
black pepper

SERVES 4

Tuscan pork and bean casserole

A 'hand' of pork is part of the shoulder of the animal. It is often considered the best part for roasting or braising, as it has just the right amount of fat, whereas the leg is so lean as to make it difficult to keep moist. Anyway, a certain amount of fat is needed in this dish to moisten the beans — or perhaps it's the other way round and the beans are needed to mop up the juices. Either way, it makes for a scrumptious dinner.

Heat the oil in a large saucepan then add the carrots, onions, turnips, thyme, bay leaf, peppercorns and garlic. Sauté gently without browning, for 10–15 minutes. Transfer to the slow cooker.

Add the pork and its rind and the bacon chunks to the slow cooker. Cover with boiling water, add salt and pepper, cover with the lid, and cook on HIGH for 3 hours. Add the cannellini beans and cook for 1 further hour. Add the potatoes for the last 30 minutes and the fresh green beans for the last 5 minutes of cooking time. (If space in your slow cooker is limited, simply cook these separately on the stovetop and serve them on the side.)

To serve, remove and discard the pork rind, lift the meat onto a dish and carve into thick slices. Add the vegetables and green beans to the dish (if cooked separately) and serve with a separate small jug/pitcher of the cooking juices.

choucroute garnie

1 kg/4 cups bottled sauerkraut

5 tablespoons goose fat or butter

250 g/9 oz. streaky bacon pieces

1 carrot, sliced

1 onion, sliced

1 fresh or dried bay leaf

2 sprigs of fresh thyme

6 peppercorns

125 ml/½ cup white wine

200 ml/¾ cup chicken stock

4 pork neck cutlets

8 frankfurters

sea salt and freshly ground
black pepper

SERVES 4

Try a choucroute at least once in your life and you'll be hooked. It reheats very well and doesn't mind waiting, so cook more than you need and have it twice. You might find goose or duck fat sold by the jar in French gourmet stores and it adds greatly to the flavour. Butter is also good, but don't use olive oil as it's completely the wrong flavour.

Drain the sauerkraut, empty it into a large saucepan and cover with water. Stir well, empty into a colander then drain. Spoon into the slow cooker.

Heat 3 tablespoons of the goose fat or butter in a large saucepan or flameproof casserole dish. Add the bacon, carrot, onion, herbs and peppercorns and cook gently for 5 minutes. Add the wine, bring to the boil and reduce by half. Add the stock and pour over the drained sauerkraut in the slow cooker.

Heat the remaining goose fat or butter in a frying pan/skillet, add the pork cutlets, season with salt and pepper and sauté until browned.

Tuck the pork cutlets into the sauerkraut, cover and cook on HIGH for 2 hours. Add the frankfurters and cook for a further 20–30 minutes. Choucroute is traditionally served on a large platter in the middle of the table.

Lancashire hotpot

500 g/1 lb. braising steak, trimmed of fat

250 g/9 oz. shoulder of lamb, trimmed of fat

2 lamb's kidneys, cleaned and trimmed (optional)

2 tablespoons plain/all-purpose flour

1 onion, thinly sliced

1 carrot, cut into chunks

1 fresh or dried bay leaf

350 g/12 oz. potatoes, cut into chunks

300 ml/1¼ cups boiling beef stock

½ teaspoon salt

1 teaspoon sugar

¼ teaspoon freshly ground black pepper

1 teaspoon anchovy essence or sauce

green beans, to serve

SERVES 4

A traditional British hotpot was an earthenware vessel with a tight-fitting lid, tall enough to take whole cuts of lamb standing upright, so it was very tall! Nowadays a slow cooker will do the job very well, as the name refers to the contents rather than the pot. The version from Lancashire in the North of England usually contains beef as well as lamb.

Cut the steak, lamb and kidneys, if using, into 3-cm/1-inch pieces and sprinkle with the flour. Arrange them in the slow cooker.

Add the onion, carrot and bay leaf then put the potatoes on top in a layer. Mix together the boiling stock with the salt, sugar, pepper and anchovy essence and pour the liquid over everything in the slow cooker. Cover with the lid and cook on HIGH for 4–5 hours.

Serve hot with green beans.

red-cooked pork

1 kg/2 lbs. pork spareribs, loin or shoulder roast, in the piece

cooked noodles or steamed rice, to serve

STOCK:

150 ml/⅔ cup Chinese rice wine

250 ml/1 cup chicken stock

150 ml/⅔ cup dark soy sauce

1 tablespoon rice vinegar

1 cinnamon stick

2-cm/1-inch piece of fresh ginger, sliced

finely grated zest/peel of 1 tangerine or small orange

1 whole star anise

3 spring onions/scallions, trimmed

SERVES 4–6

'Red-cooking' is a braising method used for whole ducks or chickens, or large pieces of pork — and the red colour comes from soy sauce. This dish uses a great deal of soy sauce, but it can be used again and again (freeze between uses). Use dark soy sauce, which is less salty than light.

Put all the stock ingredients in the slow cooker.

Add the pork, cover with the lid and cook on HIGH for 6 hours.

When the meat is very tender, carefully lift it out onto on a cutting board and cut it into thick slices or bite-size chunks. Serve with noodles or steamed rice, as preferred.

Meat cooked on the bone as it is in this recipe has a very different texture from the boned type where the meat can shrink back unimpeded into a tight ball. The meat remains stretched as it cooks and has a tender, far more open, melt-in-the-mouth texture.

braised lamb shanks with orange and marmalade

2 tablespoons olive oil

4 lamb shanks, approximately 1.5 kg/3 lbs. in total

3 garlic cloves, sliced

250 ml/1 cup fresh orange juice

100 ml/⅓ cup dry white wine

zest/peel of 1 lemon, removed with a potato peeler

3 tablespoons bitter orange marmalade

125 ml/½ cup hot chicken stock

sea salt and freshly ground black pepper

sugar snap peas and mashed swede/rutabaga, to serve (optional)

SERVES 4

Heat the olive oil in a large frying pan/skillet and add the lamb shanks. Cook for about 5 minutes, turning them as necessary, until well browned all over. Remove from the frying pan/skillet.

Add the garlic to the frying pan/skillet and brown gently without burning. Transfer the garlic and meat juices to the slow cooker and then pour in the orange juice, white wine and lemon zest/peel. Stir well. Put the lamb shanks on top of the sauce, cover with the lid, and cook on HIGH for 7–8 hours, until the meat pulls away from the bones.

Using a slotted spoon, transfer the lamb shanks to a plate or bowl and keep them warm. Transfer the sauce to a saucepan.

Add the marmalade to the saucepan and stir until well blended. Bring to the boil and simmer until the liquid has been reduced to a coating glaze. Add the lamb shanks to the saucepan and turn them in the glaze until coated. Transfer the lamb shanks to warmed servng plates. Add the stock to the saucepan, stir to scrape up the flavoured bits left in the pan, then spoon it over the shanks. Serve with green beans and mashed rutabaga, if liked.

Oxtail makes a rich stew as its natural gelatin gives the dish a deliciously sticky texture. However, it also has an excessive amount of fat on the biggest sections, most of which must be cut away before cooking and lifted off when the cooking is complete.

oxtail in red wine

6 tablespoons/⅓ cup olive oil

2 tablespoons plain/all-purpose flour

2 large onions, sliced

2 oxtails, about 2 kg/4 lbs., jointed cleanly into sections, trimmed of fat

2 carrots, cut into chunks

4 tomatoes, chopped

2–3 sprigs of fresh thyme

1 celery stalk, sliced

3 dried bay leaves

10 peppercorns

75 ml/⅓ cup brandy

375 ml/1½ cups red wine

750 ml/3 cups beef stock

sea salt and freshly ground black pepper

TO SERVE:

baby carrots and broccoli

creamy mashed potatoes

SERVES 4–6

To make a roux, put 2 tablespoons of the oil in a small saucepan, add the flour and cook gently, stirring, until it becomes a nutty brown colour. Heat another 3 tablespoons of the oil in a large frying pan/skillet, add the onions and sauté until golden. Add the smaller pieces of oxtail, carrots, tomatoes, thyme, celery, bay leaves and peppercorns. Sauté until browned. Transfer to the slow cooker.

Add the remaining oil to the frying pan/skillet and sauté the larger pieces of oxtail, until browned on all sides. Pour off the fat. Warm the brandy in a small saucepan, light with a match and pour over the meat. Shake the frying pan/skillet gently, keeping the flame alight as long as possible to burn off all the alcohol.

Transfer the meat to the slow cooker and add the wine to the frying pan/skillet. Bring to the boil and cook until it becomes syrupy and almost disappears. Stir in the roux, then the stock. Bring to the boil, stirring all the time to make a sauce. Add salt and pepper, then pour over the oxtail in the slow cooker and stir.

Cook on HIGH for 6 hours, until the meat is falling off the bone. Remove the dish from the slow cooker and set aside for about 10 minutes to let the fat rise to the surface. Spoon off as much fat as you can before serving with carrots, broccoli and plenty of mashed potatoes for mopping up the rich sauce.

Vietnamese beef

This beef casserole is eaten as street food or at home in Vietnam and is served with crusty baguettes rather than rice, a legacy of the French colonial period. Note that this recipe requires marinating for a minimum of 2 hours before it can be cooked.

1 lemon grass stalk, peeled and chopped

a few fresh mint leaves, chopped

3 tablespoons Thai fish sauce

1 teaspoon brown sugar

3-cm/1-inch piece of fresh ginger, peeled and grated

1 fresh red chilli/chile, seeded and finely chopped

2 garlic cloves, crushed

freshly ground black pepper

1 kg/2 lbs. boneless beef (shin/foreshank or chuck), cut into 2.5-cm/1-inch cubes

about 4 tablespoons/¼ cup peanut oil

2 tablespoons tomato purée/paste

400-g/14-oz. can chopped tomatoes

1 cup beef stock

TO SERVE:

6 spring onions/scallions, shredded

sprigs of fresh mint

crusty baguettes

SERVES 4–6

Put the lemon grass, mint, fish sauce, sugar, ginger, chilli/chile, garlic and lots of freshly ground black pepper in a bowl and mix well. Add the beef and turn to coat. Cover and marinate in the refrigerator for at least 2 hours or preferably overnight.

Heat the oil in a frying pan/skillet then add the beef in batches and sauté until browned on all sides. Using a slotted spoon, remove each batch to a plate and keep it warm while you cook the remainder.

Return all the beef to the frying pan/skillet, add the tomato purée/paste and tomatoes, and cook for 1–2 minutes. Add the stock and bring to the boil. Transfer to the slow cooker, cover with the lid and cook on HIGH for 4 hours, until the meat is tender.

Serve topped with shredded spring onions/scallions and mint sprigs, accompanied by crusty baguettes for mopping up the juices.

braised pork chops with tomato, orange and chilli

2 tablespoons olive oil

8 bone-in pork chops, about 280 g/
8 oz. each, trimmed

3 celery stalks, chopped

1 onion, chopped

4 garlic cloves, finely chopped

½–1 teaspoon dried red chilli/hot
pepper flakes

125 ml/½ cup full-bodied red wine,
preferably Rioja

freshly squeezed juice of 1 orange,
orange reserved

400-g/14-oz. can chopped tomatoes

1 fresh or dried bay leaf

a few sprigs of fresh oregano

sea salt

TO SERVE:

a handful of fresh flat-leaf parsley
leaves, coarsely chopped

sautéed potatoes

SERVES 4–6

*The flavours in this dish point straight to Spain,
though it is not traditional. This dish cries out
for slow cooking, because the orange, chilli and
everything else need time to mingle and develop
the flavours. It's a very homey sort of food and
perfect with potatoes, preferably sautéed.*

Heat the oil in a large frying pan/skillet. Add the pork chops and
cook for 3–5 minutes, until browned. Turn and cook the other side
(work in batches if they don't all fit in the frying pan/skillet).
Transfer to the slow cooker and season with salt.

Arrange the celery, onion, garlic and chilli/pepper flakes on top of
the chops. Pour the wine into the frying pan/skillet and stir,
scraping any bits that are stuck to the bottom of the frying
pan/skillet. Pour over the vegetables along with the orange juice
and add the tomatoes, bay leaf, oregano and salt to taste. Quarter
the orange used for the juice and tuck 1 piece into the sauce.
Cover with the lid.

Cook on HIGH for 5–6 hours, until the pork is tender, turning
the meat and sauce halfway through cooking.

Remove and discard the orange piece, bay leaf and herbs. Serve
the chops with the sauce spooned over the top and a sprinkling
of parsley leaves. Sautéed potatoes make a good accompaniment.

1 kg/2 lbs. boneless lamb, cubed

2 tablespoons olive oil

3 tablespoons plain/all-purpose flour

675 ml/2½ cups lamb stock

400-g/14-oz. can chickpeas, drained

500 g/1 lb. potatoes, peeled and cut into large chunks

500 g/1 lb. carrots, cut into large pieces

1 red (bell) pepper, seeded and cut into pieces

1 courgette/zucchini, cut into thick slices

1–2 teaspoons hot piri piri sauce

sea salt and freshly ground black pepper

couscous, to serve

MARINADE:

1 onion, chopped

6 tablespooons/⅓ cup sherry vinegar

1½ teaspoons Spanish smoked sweet paprika (pimentón dulce)

4 garlic cloves, sliced

a large handful of fresh coriander/cilantro leaves, chopped

a large handful of fresh flat-leaf parsley leaves, chopped

1 tablespoon coarse sea salt

SERVES 6

Portuguese lamb stew with piri piri

This spicy stew makes a nice change from the standard repertoire. The heat comes from Portuguese piri piri sauce, which is very hot and can vary from one brand to another, so be cautious if you've not tried it before — you can always add more sauce later if it's not hot enough. Note this recipe requires marinating for at least 3 hours before cooking.

To make the marinade, put the onion, vinegar, paprika, garlic, coriander/cilantro, parsley and salt in a large non-reactive dish. Mix well. Add the lamb and turn to coat thoroughly. Cover with clingfilm/plastic wrap and refrigerate for at least 3 hours or overnight.

Heat the oil in a large saucepan. When hot, add the lamb and all the marinade. Cook for 5–8 minutes, until the lamb is well sealed. Sprinkle with the flour, stir to coat well and cook for 1–2 minutes. Pour in the stock and chickpeas, stir well and bring to the boil.

Put the potatoes and carrots in the bottom of the slow cooker. Spoon over the lamb, stock and chickpea mixture (not stirring into vegetables underneath) then cover with the lid and cook on HIGH for 4 hours. Remove the lid, add the (bell) pepper, courgette/zucchini, piri piri and seasoning, cover and cook for 1 further hour.

Remove the lid, stir well and if the sauce is a little watery, simmer for a further 10–15 minutes with the lid off. Adjust the seasoning to taste and serve with couscous.

10–12 thin slices of beef, rump, or topside

10–12 slices of cured ham, such as prosciutto

1 tablespoon olive oil

TOMATO SAUCE:

2 tablespoons extra virgin olive oil

1 celery stalk, chopped

1 carrot, chopped

1 onion, chopped

2 garlic cloves, crushed

125 ml/½ cup dry white wine

400-g/14-oz. can whole plum tomatoes

a small bunch of fresh thyme sprigs, tied with kitchen twine

sea salt and freshly ground black pepper

STUFFING:

4–6 garlic cloves, crushed

a handful of fresh flat-leaf parsley leaves, finely chopped

fresh breadcrumbs (allow 1 tablespoon per slice of beef)

2 tablespoons olive oil, plus extra for browning

sea salt and freshly ground black pepper

cocktail sticks/toothpicks or kitchen twine

SERVES 4

beef rolls with cured ham in tomato sauce

This recipe combines the best of both French and Italian cuisines. The garlic-parsley filling is French and the cured ham and tomato sauce is more like the Italian dish, involtini.

To make the sauce, heat the oil in a frying pan/skillet. Add the celery, carrot and onion and cook for 3–5 minutes, until just browning and aromatic. Stir in the garlic, season lightly and cook for 1 minute. Stir in the wine, scraping up any bits that stick to the frying pan/skillet and boil for 1 minute. Add the tomatoes, thyme and a pinch of salt. Stir well, then simmer gently while you prepare the meat.

To make the stuffing, put the garlic in a bowl (4 cloves for 8–10 rolls, 6 for more) with the parsley, breadcrumbs, oil, a pinch of salt and some pepper. Mix well. If you are making 12 rolls, you may need a bit more oil. Set aside.

Working on one at a time, put the beef slices between 2 sheets of clingfim/plastic wrap and roll with a rolling pin until thin — a few holes are fine, but not too many. Still working on one at a time, set a flattened slice of beef on a work surface. Top with a slice of ham and sprinkle with a spoonful of the stuffing. Roll up from the short end and secure with a cocktail stick/toothpick or kitchen twine. Repeat until all the beef has been used. Set aside.

Heat the oil in a large shallow frying pan/skillet. Add the beef rolls and cook for 3–5 minutes, until brown on all sides. Transfer to the slow cooker. Pour in the tomato sauce and spread evenly. Cover with the lid and cook on HIGH for 4 hours. Remove the lid halfway through the cooking time and stir. Serve hot.

50 g/1 cup fresh breadcrumbs

3 tablespoons milk

1 small onion, finely chopped

a handful of fresh flat-leaf parsley leaves, chopped

2 garlic cloves, crushed

800 g/1¾ cups mince/ground meat, preferably a mix of beef and pork

1½ teaspoons fine sea salt

1 teaspoon dried oregano

1 teaspoon ground cumin

½ teaspoon paprika

1 egg, beaten

RED PEPPER SAUCE:

several sprigs of fresh thyme

1 fresh or dried bay leaf

2 tablespoons olive oil

1 onion, grated

6 garlic cloves, crushed

¼ teaspoon cayenne pepper

5 tablespoons/⅓ cup red wine

½ unwaxed orange, well scrubbed

1 litre/4 cups passata (Italian strained tomatoes)

½ a large jar roasted red (bell) peppers, drained and chopped

sea salt and freshly ground black pepper

kitchen twine

MAKES ABOUT 25 MEATBALLS

meatballs in red pepper sauce

This is great family food, best served with sautéed potatoes. Should you have any leftover, it makes a great sandwich filling. If you don't have time to make the sauce, substitute prepared pasta sauce for speed (you'll need two 500-g/1-lb. jars).

To make the red (bell) pepper sauce, tie up the thyme and bay leaf with kitchen twine. Heat the oil in a frying pan/skillet. Add the onion and a pinch of salt and cook for 2–3 minutes, until soft. Add the garlic and cayenne and cook, stirring, for 1 minute. Stir in the wine and squeeze in the orange juice (reserve the rest of the orange) and cook for 30 seconds. Add the passata, a good pinch of salt, the bunch of herbs and the reserved orange. Simmer gently for 20–30 minutes, until thick. Season to taste with salt and pepper. Stir in the red (bell) peppers, remove the herbs and orange and leave the sauce until needed. It can be made a day ahead.

To make the meatballs, put the breadcrumbs, milk, onion, parsley, garlic, minced/ground meat, salt, oregano, cumin, paprika and beaten egg in a large bowl. Mix well (your hands are best). Shape spoonfuls of the meat mixture into balls, just slightly larger than a golf ball.

Put the meatballs in the slow cooker, pour over the reheated homemade or prepared sauce and gently stir to coat the meatballs, taking care not to break them. Cover with the lid and cook on HIGH for 2 hours. Shake the cooker from time to time to keep the meatballs separate.

This is a cheat's version of a Spanish peasant stew called a fabada — beans, sausage and a rich tomato and red wine sauce make a welcoming supper to come home to on a cold winter's evening. If you can't get hold of chorizo, any spicy sausage will do.

sausage and butter bean stew

2 tablespoons olive oil

2 onions, finely chopped

4 garlic cloves, crushed

200 g/6½ oz. chorizo sausage, skin removed and cut into 1-cm/½-inch slices

200 ml/¾ cup red wine

3 x 400-g/14-oz. cans chopped tomatoes

2 red onions, cut into thin petals

3 x 400-g/14-oz. cans butter beans, drained

2 teaspoon dried mixed herbs

a few sprigs of fresh rosemary or thyme

sea salt and freshly ground black pepper

4 tablespoons freshly grated Parmesan cheese

warm crusty bread, to serve

SERVES 6

Heat the oil in a large, high-sided frying pan/skillet. Add the onion and garlic and cook for a few minutes over medium heat. Add the chorizo sausage and cook for a further 2–3 minutes. Add the red wine and bring to the boil.

Transfer to the slow cooker, adding the tomatoes, red onion petals, butter beans, 100 ml/⅓ cup water, the dried mixed herbs and rosemary or thyme sprigs.

Cover with the lid and cook on HIGH for 2 hours.

Season to taste with salt and pepper and spoon into warmed serving bowls. Sprinkle with the Parmesan cheese and serve immediately with chunks of warm crusty bread to mop up the rich juices.

700 g/1¾ lbs. boneless shoulder of
lamb, trimmed and cut into 5-cm/
2-inch cubes

3 tablespoons olive oil

1 large onion, thinly sliced

2 garlic cloves, finely chopped

4 large tomatoes, peeled, seeded
and chopped

200 ml/¾ cup vegetable stock

2 dried bay leaves

2 green (bell) peppers, seeded and
thickly sliced

500 g/1 lb. carrots, thickly sliced

180 g/6 oz. dried apricots

handful of coriander/cilantro leaves

CHERMOULA PASTE:

1 teaspoon ground cumin

1 teaspoon ground coriander

a pinch of saffron threads

2 garlic cloves, chopped

1 teaspoon finely grated lemon
zest/peel

1 teaspoon mild paprika

2 tablespoons chopped fresh
flat-leaf parsley

3 tablespoons chopped fresh
coriander/cilantro

freshly squeezed juice of 1 lemon

4 tablespoons olive oil

chilli/chili powder, to taste

sea salt and freshly ground
black pepper

SERVES 4

*This Moroccan-style stew (tagine) is heady with
spices, herbs and dried fruit. The chermoula paste
may have a long list of ingredients but is very quick
to make and well worth the effort. Serve with either a
rice pilaf or couscous to soak up the delicious juices.*

Moroccan lamb stew with chermoula

To make the chermoula, put the cumin, ground coriander and
saffron in a small saucepan and heat gently for 1 minute until
aromatic. Transfer to a food processor, then add the garlic, lemon
zest/peel, paprika, parsley and coriander/cilantro and finely chop.
Add the lemon juice and oil and blend. Add a little chilli powder,
salt and pepper to taste. Cover and set aside for 30 minutes.

Put the lamb and half the chermoula paste in a non-reactive
bowl, toss well to coat, then cover and let marinate in the fridge
for 2–12 hours (keep the remaining chermoula in the fridge too).

Scrape the chermoula off of the lamb and reserve it. Heat
2 tablespoons of the oil in a large frying pan/skillet. Add the meat
and brown on all sides over medium-high heat. Put the meat into
the slow cooker when browned.

Heat the remaining oil in the frying pan/skillet, add the onion and
cook gently for 10–15 minutes, until softened and just beginning
to brown. Add the garlic and the chermoula marinade from the
lamb and cook for a few more minutes over medium heat. Put the
onion mixture along with the rest of the ingredients in the slow
cooker, cover with the lid and cook on HIGH for 6–7 hours. Stir
in the remaining chermoula, check the seasoning and cook for a
further 20 minutes. Serve sprinkled with the coriander/cilantro.

2 tablespoons safflower oil

800 g/1¾ lbs. boneless lamb shoulder, cut into large bite-size pieces

2 large onions, thickly sliced

3 garlic cloves, crushed

2 teaspoons finely grated fresh ginger

2 cinnamon sticks

2 teaspoons chilli powder

2 teaspoons paprika

6 cardamom pods

4 tablespoons medium curry paste

400-g/14-oz. can chopped tomatoes

6 tablespoons tomato purée/paste

1 teaspoon sugar

150 ml/⅔ cup lamb stock

4–6 potatoes, peeled and left whole

a handful of chopped fresh coriander/cilantro leaves

plain yogurt, to serve

SERVES 4

lamb rogan josh

This slow-cooked lamb stew from Kashmir in north India is perfect for hassle-free entertaining as it almost cooks itself!

Heat 1 tablespoon of the safflower oil in a large casserole dish or heavy-based saucepan. Add the lamb in batches and cook for 3–4 minutes, until evenly browned. Remove with a slotted spoon and transfer to the slow cooker.

Add the remaining oil to the casserole and add the onions. Cook over medium heat for 10–12 minutes, stirring often until soft and lightly browned. Add the garlic, ginger, cinnamon, chilli powder, paprika and cardamom pods. Stir-fry for 1–2 minutes, then add the curry paste. Stir-fry for 2–3 minutes, then stir in the canned tomatoes, tomato purée/paste, sugar, stock and potatoes. Season well, bring to the boil, and pour over the lamb in the slow cooker. Cook on HIGH for 7–8 hours. To serve, sprinkle with the chopped coriander/cilantro and drizzle with yogurt.

beef and pea curry

2 tablespoons safflower oil

1 large onion, finely chopped

3 garlic cloves, crushed

1 teaspoon finely grated fresh ginger

2 fresh green chillies/chiles, seeded and thinly sliced

1 tablespoon cumin seeds

4 tablespoons medium curry paste

800 g/1¾ lbs. minced/ground beef

400-g/14-oz. can chopped tomatoes

1 teaspoon sugar

4 tablespoons/¼ cup tomato purée/paste

4 tablespoons/¼ cup coconut cream

250 g/8 oz. frozen peas

salt and freshly ground black pepper

3 tablespoons chopped fresh coriander/cilantro leaves

steamed basmati rice, to serve

SERVES 4

Minced/ground beef is cooked slowly with spices and peas resulting in a subtle, fragrant curry which is great accompanied by steamed basmati rice or bread.

Heat the safflower oil in a large, heavy-based saucepan and add the onion. Cook over low heat for 15 minutes, until softened and just turning light golden.

Add the garlic, ginger, chillies/chiles, cumin seeds and curry paste and stir-fry over high heat for 1–2 minutes. Add the minced/ground beef and stir-fry for 3–4 minutes until the meat is browned, then stir in the canned tomatoes, sugar, tomato purée/paste and 100 ml/⅓ cup cold water and bring to the boil. Transfer to the slow cooker, season, cover with the lid, and cook on HIGH for 5 hours. Stir in the coconut cream and peas 1 hour before the end of cooking time.

Sprinkle with the chopped coriander/cilantro and serve with steamed basmati rice.

beef madras

This fiery curry from southern India is not for the faint-hearted although you can decrease the amounts of chilli/chile and curry powder to suit your palate. Serve with pickles as well as steamed basmati rice.

800 g/1¾ lbs. stewing beef, cut into large bite-size pieces

2 tablespoons safflower oil

1 large onion, thinly sliced

3 garlic cloves, crushed

1 tablespoon finely grated fresh ginger

1 teaspoon ground turmeric

1 fresh red chilli/chile, split in half lengthways

2 teaspoons hot chilli/chili powder

2 teaspoons ground cumin

200 g/7 oz. canned chopped tomatoes

300 g/1¼ cups coconut milk, plus extra to drizzle

¼ teaspoon garam masala

salt and freshly ground black pepper

a small handful of fresh coriander/cilantro leaves, chopped

steamed basmati rice and poppadoms, to serve

MARINADE:

5 tablespoons plain yogurt (not low fat)

3 tablespoons Madras curry paste

SERVES 4

To make the marinade, combine the yogurt and curry paste in a glass bowl. Stir in the beef, season with salt, cover and let marinate in the fridge for at least 30 minutes.

Heat the safflower oil in a large nonstick frying pan/skillet and add the onion. Stir-fry over medium heat for 4–5 minutes, then add the garlic, ginger, turmeric, red chilli/chile, chilli powder and cumin. Add the beef and stir-fry for 5 minutes, until the meat is sealed.

Transfer the meat mixture to the slow cooker and add the canned tomatoes. Cover with the lid and cook on HIGH for 7 hours. Stir in the coconut milk and garam masala 5 minutes before the end of the cooking time. Season to taste, drizzle with coconut milk and garnish with the chopped coriander/cilantro. Serve with steamed basmati rice and poppadoms.

lamb and butternut squash stew

800 g/1¾ lbs. stewing lamb, cubed

3 tablespoons plain/all-purpose flour seasoned with salt and pepper

1 teaspoon cumin seeds

1 teaspoon fennel seeds

6 tablespoons olive oil

1 onion, chopped

1 small butternut squash, peeled, deseeded and cubed

400 ml/1½ cups lamb or vegetable stock

a pinch of saffron threads

1 cinnamon stick

1 whole garlic bulb, separated

leaves from a bunch of fresh coriander/cilantro, chopped

SERVES 4

This is a deliciously different stew that is very simple to make but tastes quite exotic. Serve with plenty of buttery couscous and a crispy salad.

Place the lamb in a plastic bag with the seasoned flour and shake to coat well.

Toast the cumin and fennel seeds for 1–2 minutes in a small, dry frying pan/skillet set over medium heat, until fragrant.

Heat 4 tablespoons of the oil in a large casserole dish or heavy-based saucepan. Add the lamb and fry in batches until brown all over, then remove from the frying pan/skillet. Add the remaining oil and fry the onion for 2–3 minutes, until soft. Add the butternut squash and cook for 3–4 minutes. Return the lamb to the pan and pour in the stock. Add the toasted spices, saffron, cinnamon and separated garlic cloves (there is no need to peel them). Bring to the boil, then transfer to the slow cooker. Cook on HIGH for 3–4 hours, until the lamb is tender.

Stir in the chopped coriander/cilantro and serve with couscous.

Tip
Do try squeezing the softened garlic out of its skin and smearing it on the tender chunks of lamb.

A tagine is a Moroccan stew that's traditionally cooked in a large-lidded terracotta pot, which gives the dish its name. Like all stews made with aromatic spices, this tastes even better the next day, once the flavours have mingled, so it's perfect for cooking in the slow cooker overnight — simply reheat when you are ready to serve the following evening.

1.25 kg/2¾ lbs. boneless shoulder of lamb or shoulder chops, cut into large chunks

2 teaspoons ground cinnamon

2 teaspoons ground cumin

½ teaspoon hot chilli/chili powder

1 teaspoon ground turmeric

a pinch of saffron threads

½ teaspoon ground white pepper

4 tablespoons olive oil

3 onions, chopped

3 garlic cloves, crushed

400 ml/1½ cups hot lamb or vegetable stock

200 g/1 cup fava beans, podded

150 g/1 cup dates, pitted

a handful of fresh coriander/cilantro leaves, roughly chopped

couscous, to serve

SERVES 4

lamb and fava bean tagine

Put the lamb in a large bowl and toss with the cinnamon, cumin, chilli powder, turmeric, saffron and pepper.

Heat 2 tablespoons of the olive oil in a frying pan/skillet set over medium heat, then add half the lamb. Cook for 2–3 minutes, stirring occasionally, until the lamb is evenly browned. Tip into a bowl, add more oil to the pan and brown the remainder of the lamb. Remove and then add the onions and garlic. Stir-fry for a few minutes until softened. Return the lamb to the pan and add the stock and a large pinch of salt. Bring the mixture to the boil, then transfer it to the slow cooker. Cover with the lid and cook on HIGH for 1 hour then stir in the fava beans. Cook on HIGH for 1 further hour before adding the dates, then cook on HIGH for 1–2 hours, until the meat is so tender that it falls apart easily.

Sprinkle over the chopped coriander/cilantro and serve with couscous.

beef daube

750 g/1½ lbs. chuck steak, in one piece

1 large carrot, diced

1 celery stalk, diced

1 fresh or dried bay leaf

3 garlic cloves, unpeeled and smashed

500 ml/2 cups red wine

400 g/14-oz. can chopped tomatoes

250 ml/1 cup beef stock

400 g/14 oz. dried rigatoni or penne

130 g/1 cup frozen baby peas, thawed

50 g/½ cup finely grated Parmesan cheese

sea salt and freshly ground black pepper

SERVES 6–8

This is definitely not fast food, so relax and let the ingredients and your slow cooker do all the work. You can use a cheaper cut of meat here and it will still taste good after a long marinating and cooking time.

Put the beef in the slow cooker dish with the carrot, celery, bay leaf, garlic and red wine. Cover with the lid and refrigerate overnight, turning occasionally.

Remove from the fridge and pour in the tomatoes and stock. Cover with the lid. Cook on HIGH for 5–6 hours, until the meat is tender. Remove the meat from the dish and roughly shred it with a fork. Return the meat to the dish and season to taste with salt and pepper.

Stir in the pasta, replace the lid and cook on HIGH for a further 20 minutes. Stir in the peas, cover with the lid and cook for a further 10 minutes until the pasta is tender and the peas hot. Serve with a sprinkle of grated Parmesan.

lamb kefta meatballs

500 g/1 lb. minced/ground lamb

1 large onion, grated or very finely chopped

2 garlic cloves, finely chopped

a handful of fresh flat-leaf parsley leaves, finely chopped

beaten egg, to bind

plain/all-purpose flour, to dust

4 tablespoons olive oil

1 teaspoon ground cumin

1 teaspoon ground cinnamon

400 g/14-oz. can chopped tomatoes

½ teaspoon cayenne pepper

a large handful of fresh coriander/cilantro leaves, chopped

crunchy salad and pita bread, to serve

SERVES 4

If you are interested in cooking with spices, Moroccan food is a great place to start. This style of cooking uses a relatively short list of staple spices, such as cumin, cinnamon and cayenne pepper, but they are all used in varying quantities to produce very different results from one recipe to the next.

Put the lamb, half of the onion, half of the garlic and all the parsley in a bowl and add a little beaten egg to bind. Use your hands to combine and throw the mixture against the side of the bowl several times. Then, using lightly floured hands, divide the mixture into approximately 24 walnut-size balls. Toss each in a little flour to lightly coat, cover and chill in the fridge.

Heat half of the oil in a large, heavy-based frying pan/skillet set over high heat. Add the remaining onion and garlic and cook for 3–4 minutes, until softened and golden. Add the spices and cook, stirring constantly, for 1 minute, until aromatic. Add the tomatoes and 250 ml/1 cup water and bring to the boil. Transfer the tomato sauce to the slow cooker.

Heat the remaining olive oil in a large frying pan/skillet set over medium heat. Add the meatballs and fry for 3–5 minutes, turning frequently until well browned. Transfer the meatballs to the tomato sauce in the slow cooker, cover with the lid, and cook on HIGH for 3 hours. Stir in the cayenne pepper and cook for 1 hour further. (Cayenne can become bitter if cooked for too long a time.)

Serve with crunchy salad and pita bread.

lamb shanks in red wine with cannellini beans

2 trimmed lamb shanks, about 400 g/14 oz. each

30 g/2 oz. pancetta, chopped

400 g/14-oz. can chopped tomatoes in rich juice

200 ml/¾ cup beef stock

150 ml/⅔ cup red wine

1 tablespoon sun-dried tomato purée/paste

1 fresh or dried bay leaf

2 sprigs of fresh thyme

a handful of fresh flat-leaf parsley, finely chopped

400 g/14-oz. can cannellini beans, drained and rinsed

sea salt and freshly ground black pepper

SERVES 4

Lamb shanks have recently become popular again but at one time they were trimmed off and discarded by the butcher. It's great that they are enjoying a revival, as they make the ideal ingredient for cooking in a slow cooker. This is great for winter entertaining; perfect comfort food for hungry guests.

Put the lamb shanks in the slow cooker. Add the pancetta, canned tomatoes, stock, red wine, sun-dried tomato purée/paste, bay leaf, thyme and half of the parsley. Season well with salt and pepper, stir to combine and cover with the lid.

Cook on HIGH for 3½ hours then turn the shanks over, add the cannellini beans, and cook for a further 1½ hours, until the mixture is thick and the lamb is very tender.

Spoon a quarter of the beans into each dish, add a lamb shank, and spoon some sauce over the top. Sprinkle with the remaining parsley and serve.

Like many classic, handed-down recipes, there are countless versions of Bolognese sauce. Some Italian chefs add sweetbreads, chicken livers and veal, but here this homey recipe uses a mixture of minced/ground beef and Parma ham. It really benefits from being chilled overnight, so it's ideal for making the day before; gently reheat when you are ready to serve.

rich Bolognese sauce

15 g/½ oz. dried porcini mushrooms, rinsed

1 tablespoon olive oil

1 onion, finely chopped

450 g/1 lb. minced/ground beef

50 g/2 oz. Parma ham or prosciutto, coarsely chopped

80 ml/⅓ cup Marsala or sherry

680 ml/2¾ cups passata (Italian strained tomatoes)

salt and freshly ground black pepper

dried spaghetti or linguine, to serve

shavings of fresh Parmesan cheese, to serve

SERVES 4

Put the porcini into a bowl, cover with boiling water and set aside for 20 minutes until softened.

Heat the oil in a large saucepan, add the onion and cook for 2 minutes. Add the beef and Parma ham and cook for about 3–4 minutes, stirring, until evenly browned.

Drain the porcini and discard the soaking water. Chop the porcini, then add to the pan with the Marsala and passata. Bring to the boil and transfer to the slow cooker. Cover with the lid and cook on HIGH for 4 hours. Remove the lid for the last 30 minutes of cooking time to reduce and thicken the sauce. Add salt and pepper to taste.

Cook the pasta according to the package instructions. Drain well and divide between serving plates or bowls. Top with the Bolognese sauce and Parmesan shavings, to serve.

The traditional way to eat this in Italy would be to serve the sauce with the pasta and to follow with the steak, a selection of salads, and some crusty bread. Here the steak is cut into slices and mixed with the pasta and sauce to make a delicious one-bowl meal.

Italian steak sauce

1 tablespoon chopped fresh rosemary needles

2 tablespoons chopped fresh flat-leaf parsley, plus extra to serve

2 garlic cloves, crushed

4 sun-dried or sun-blush tomatoes

2 teaspoons capers, drained

8 x 50-g/2-oz. minute steaks

1 tablespoon olive oil

2 x 400 g/14-oz. cans plum tomatoes

300 g/10 oz. dried conchiglie or rigatoni

300 ml/1¼ cups boiling water

salt and freshly ground black pepper

kitchen twine

SERVES 4

Put the rosemary, parsley, garlic, sun-dried tomatoes and capers into a small food processor and blend until finely chopped.

Put the steaks onto a work surface and sprinkle lightly with salt and freshly ground black pepper. Spread the herb mixture evenly over each steak and roll up tightly, tying twine around the middle to secure.

Heat the olive oil until very hot in a large sauté pan, add the rolled steaks and cook for 2–3 minutes until browned all over. Transfer to the slow cooker and add the canned tomatoes and salt and pepper to taste. Cover with the lid and cook on HIGH for 1 hour. After 1 hour add the pasta and boiling water and cook for a further 25–30 minutes, until the pasta is cooked.

Transfer the steaks from the slow cooker to a chopping board. Remove and discard the twine, then cut each steak crossways into chunky slices. Return the sliced steaks to the pasta and sauce and mix together.

Divide between bowls or plates, top with the extra chopped parsley and serve.

lamb shanks with red wine, rosemary and garlic

6 even-size lamb shanks, about 2 kg/4½ lbs. in total

1 large onion, thinly sliced

3 carrots, cut into thin batons

4 garlic cloves, thinly sliced

2–3 sprigs of fresh rosemary

½ teaspoon black peppercorns

500 ml/2 cups red wine, such as Shiraz, Malbec or Zinfandel

4 tablespoons olive oil

500 ml/2 cups passata (Italian strained tomatoes)

tomato ketchup, to taste

sea salt and freshly ground black pepper

creamy mashed potatoes, to serve

a large, strong plastic bag

SERVES 6

Believe it or not, the preparation and cooking of this dish can be spread over three days, which makes it the perfect dish to serve for Sunday lunch. Start marinating the meat on Friday evening, cook it on Saturday, then simply reheat it on Sunday.

Put the lamb shanks in the large, strong plastic bag. Add the onion, carrots, garlic, rosemary and peppercorns. Pour in the bottle of wine, then pull up the sides of the bag so the marinade covers the meat. Secure the top of the bag with a wire twist. Put the bag in a bowl or dish and refrigerate overnight.

The next day, remove the lamb shanks from the marinade, pat them dry with paper towels and season with salt and pepper. Reserve the vegetables and marinade.

Heat half of the oil in a large flameproof casserole dish, add the lamb shanks and brown them thoroughly on all sides — you may need to do this in batches. Transfer the lamb shanks to the slow cooker. Add the remaining oil to the casserole dish, then add the reserved vegetables and fry briefly until they begin to soften. Add the reserved marinade and bubble for about 5 minutes, incorporating any caramelized juices that have stuck to the casserole dish. Stir in the passata then pour over the lamb shanks in the slow cooker. Cook on HIGH for 7–8 hours.

Skim off any fat from the surface of the sauce then season to taste with salt and pepper and sweeten with a little tomato ketchup, if necessary. Serve with creamy mashed potatoes.

osso buco-style veal chops

4 large veal chops, about 1 kg/2 lbs. in total

2 tablespoons olive oil

2 tablespoons butter

1 small onion, finely chopped

1 celery stalk, thinly sliced

2 garlic cloves, crushed

150 ml/⅔ cup Italian dry white wine, such as Pinot Grigio

150 ml/⅔ cup passata (Italian strained tomatoes)

50 ml/¼ cup vegetable or chicken stock

boiled white rice

GREEN OLIVE GREMOLATA:

finely grated zest/peel of 1 lemon

10 pitted green olives, finely chopped

3 heaped tablespoons finely chopped fresh parsley

SERVES 4

Osso buco is one of those dishes about which huge arguments rage. Whether there should be tomato or no tomato. At what stage you should add the gremolata (the parsley, lemon and garlic topping). Whether it should be cooked for one hour or three. The only thing Italians seem to be able to agree on is that it should contain veal and white wine.

Trim any excess fat from the chops. Heat a large, shallow frying pan/skillet and add the oil. Heat for 1 minute, then add the butter. When the foaming has subsided, add the veal chops and fry them for about 3 minutes on each side until nicely browned. Remove the chops from the pan and place in the slow cooker.

Add the onion and celery to the pan and cook over low heat for 5–6 minutes, until softened. Stir in the garlic, then increase the heat to high and pour in the wine. Let it bubble up for a few minutes until the wine has reduced by half, then add the passata and stock. Stir well, then pour over the chops in the slow cooker. Cover with the lid and cook on HIGH for 2½ hours.

To prepare the gremolata, put the lemon zest/peel, olives and parsley in a bowl and mix well.

Add half of the gremolata to the chops in the slow cooker and cook for a further 15 minutes. Transfer the chops to serving plates, spoon the sauce over the top and sprinkle with the remaining gremolata. Serve immediately with rice.

3 tablespoons peanut or vegetable oil

750 g/1½ lbs. well trimmed boneless pork sparerib, sliced into chunks

350 ml/1½ cups beef stock

CURRY PASTE (HINLEH):

4–6 fresh red bird's eye chillies/ chiles, seeded and chopped

5 garlic cloves, quartered

½ onion, coarsely chopped

5-cm/2-inch piece of fresh ginger, peeled and grated

¼ teaspoon ground turmeric

5-cm/2-inch piece of fresh galangal, peeled and grated

1 lemon grass stalk, outer leaves discarded, the remainder very finely chopped

3 anchovies in oil, drained and finely chopped

1 tablespoon Thai fish sauce

TO SERVE:

a handful of fresh coriander/cilantro leaves

2 fresh red bird's eye chillies/chiles, finely sliced lengthways

boiled basmati rice

SERVES 4

This curry is a Burmese speciality and doesn't include coconut milk (so typical of South-east Asian cooking), which makes it more suitable for preparing in a slow cooker. Boneless sparerib meat gives the best results at a lower temperature so do look out for it. If you can't get fresh galangal, use extra fresh ginger instead.

Burmese pork hinleh

To make the curry paste, put all the ingredients in a small food processor and blend to a paste, adding a dash of water to help the blades run. Heat the oil in a large saucepan and add the curry paste. Stir-fry for 5 minutes. Add the pork and stir-fry to seal.

Transfer the pork to the slow cooker, add the stock, cover with the lid, and cook on HIGH for 7 hours until very tender. Sprinkle with the coriander/cilantro and chilli/chile and serve with rice.

cassoulet

250 g/9 oz. smoked Italian pancetta

4 tablespoons olive oil

4 boneless duck breasts, halved crossways, or chicken legs or thighs

400 g/14 oz. fresh Toulouse sausages or Italian coarse pork sausages, cut into 3 pieces each

2 onions, chopped

1 large carrot, chopped

4–6 large garlic cloves, crushed

1 fresh or dried bay leaf

1 teaspoon dried thyme

1 whole clove

2 tablespoons tomato purée/paste

6 sun-dried tomatoes in oil, drained and coarsely chopped

2 x 400 g/14-oz. cans haricot/navy beans, drained and rinsed

400 ml/1½ cups hot chicken stock

sea salt and freshly ground black pepper

BREADCRUMB TOPPING:

75 g/1 cup fresh white breadcrumbs

25 g/4 tablespoons unsalted butter, melted (optional)

SERVES 4

This hearty dish from south-west France is a firm family favourite. It is big and filling, and traditionally made with a type of haricot/navy bean (lingots) instead of butter beans. It reheats very well (top up with a little more liquid if it looks dry) and is a boon for entertaining vast numbers without fuss. Make this for large gatherings on cold winter days.

Trim and discard the rind from the pancetta, and cut the flesh into large pieces. Heat 2 tablespoons of the oil in a frying pan/skillet, brown the pieces in batches and transfer to a plate. Heat the remaining oil in the pan, add the duck breasts and fry skin side down until the skin is golden. Transfer to the same plate as the pancetta. Brown the sausages in the same way and add to the plate. Add the onions to the pan, then the carrot, garlic, bay leaf, dried thyme, clove, tomato purée/paste and sun-dried tomatoes. Cook for 5 minutes until soft.

To assemble the dish, put half the beans in the slow cooker. Add an even layer of all the meats, then the onion and tomato mixture. Season well with salt and pepper. Cover with the remaining beans, and then pour over the hot stock. Cover with the lid and cook on HIGH for 6 hours.

To make the topping, combine the breadcrumbs with the melted butter. Put on a baking sheet and toast in a preheated oven at 180°C (350°F) Gas 4 for about 15–20 minutes, until crisp and golden. Sprinkle the breadcrumbs over the top of the cassoulet and serve. Alternatively, omit the butter and dry-fry the breadcrumbs in a small frying pan/skillet.

1 onion, coarsely chopped

4 garlic cloves, coarsely chopped

1 red (bell) pepper, halved, seeded and coarsely chopped

1 fresh red chilli/chile, seeded and chopped

2 teaspoons mild chilli/chili powder

1 teaspoon sweet paprika

1 teaspoon ground cumin

1 teaspoon ground coriander

½ teaspoon ground cinnamon

1 teaspoon dried oregano

150 ml/⅔ cup lager beer

500 g/1 lb. pork steaks

4 tablespoons safflower oil

200-g/7-oz. can chopped tomatoes

150 ml/⅔ cup tomato juice or passata (Italian strained tomatoes)

25 g/1 oz. very dark chocolate, chopped or ½ tablespoon unsweetened cocoa powder

400 g/14-oz. can pinto beans or black-eyed beans/peas, drained and rinsed

sea salt and freshly ground black pepper

TO SERVE:

fresh tomato and red onion salsa

chopped avocado or guacamole

sour cream

soft flour tortillas or rice

SERVES 4–6

Mexican pork and beans in red chilli/chile sauce

This version of chilli is not too spicy, made with pork, not beef, and just a few beans, then enriched Mexican-style with a little chocolate for depth. Serve it with generous bowls of a simple fresh tomato and red onion salsa, chopped avocado, sour cream, a pile of warmed soft tortillas or a big bowl of rice for a great family feast.

Put the onion, garlic, red (bell) pepper, chilli/chile, chilli powder, paprika, cumin, coriander, cinnamon and oregano in a food processor. Add half the lager and blend to a smooth purée.

Trim the pork steaks, then cut into large pieces. Working in batches, heat the oil in a large frying pan/skillet, add the pork and fry until browned. Transfer to a plate.

Add the purée to the pan and cook, stirring continuously, over moderate heat for 5 minutes — make sure it doesn't catch and burn, but it should start to caramelize. Stir in the tomatoes, tomato juice, pork and the juices. Season with salt and pepper and bring to the boil. Transfer to the slow cooker, cover with the lid and cook on HIGH or 2 hours. Stir in the chocolate and beans and cook for 1 further hour.

Serve with the accompaniments of your choice.

beef and carrot casserole with cheese dumplings

800 g/1¾ lbs. chuck steak, cut into cubes

2 tablespoons plain/all-purpose flour seasoned with salt and pepper

4 tablespoons olive oil

1 onion, diced

2 garlic cloves, crushed

2 celery stalks, diced

4 carrots, cut into small chunks

300 ml/1¼ cups beef stock

150 ml/⅔ cup red wine

2 dried bay leaves

sea salt and freshly ground black pepper

CHEESE DUMPLINGS:

1 teaspoon baking powder

200 g/1⅔ cups plain/all-purpose flour

75 g/3 oz. solid vegetable shortening, such as Trex/Crisco

75 g/3 oz. mature/sharp Cheddar cheese, grated

SERVES 4–6

Think of chilly, dark evenings and this is exactly what you'd want to eat. The feather-light dumplings nestling in the rich, savoury casserole will have everyone asking for second helpings.

Place the beef in a strong plastic bag with the seasoned flour and shake to coat well.

Heat 3 tablespoons of the oil in a large frying pan/skillet. Add the beef and fry in batches, until brown all over, then remove from the frying pan/skillet. Add the remaining oil and fry the onion, garlic, celery and carrots for 2–3 minutes, until soft. Add the stock, red wine, seasoning and bay leaves. Bring to the boil, then transfer to the slow cooker. Cover with the lid and cook on HIGH for 2–3 hours.

To make the dumplings, put the flour and baking powder in a bowl and rub in the vegetable fat until it resembles breadcrumbs. Add the cheese, mixing it in with a knife. Add a scant 75–100 ml/⅓ cup of cold water and use your hands to bring the mixture together and form a dough. Divide the dough into 8 pieces of equal size and roll them into balls. Place the dumplings on top of the casserole, re-cover with the lid, and cook on HIGH for 1 further hour.

1 onion, chopped

1 carrot, chopped

2 garlic cloves, crushed

1 celery stalk, finely chopped

450 g/1 lb. lean minced/ground beef

400 g/14-oz. can cherry tomatoes
(or regular chopped tomatoes)

300 ml/1¼ cups beef stock

2 tablespoons tomato purée/paste

1 teaspoon sugar

1 teaspoon mixed dried herbs

sea salt and freshly ground
black pepper

TO SERVE:

320 g/12 oz. dried tagliatelle

freshly grated Parmesan cheese

SERVES 4

tagliatelle with rich meat sauce

This is a lovely, easy sauce that bubbles away in your slow cooker to become deliciously sticky. It's a little like a Bolognese but makes a nice change.

Place all the sauce ingredients in the slow cooker, breaking up the beef into pieces with a wooden spoon. Cover with the lid. Cook on HIGH for 5 hours. Add the pasta, stir into the sauce and cook for a further 30 minutes until tender.

Alternatively, if time is short, cook the pasta according to the package instructions in a separate saucepan and drain well. Toss with the sauce.

Serve immediately, sprinkled generously with freshly grated Parmesan and extra black pepper.

poultry
& game

chicken and bacon pot

300 g/10 oz. thick bacon, diced

250 g/8 oz. button mushrooms

4 skinless chicken breasts

1 tablespoon olive oil

1 tablespoon butter

1 garlic clove, crushed

2 shallots, diced

3 tablespoons plain/all-purpose flour

500 ml/2 cups chicken stock

200 ml/¾ cup white wine

1 fresh or dried bay leaf

sea salt and freshly ground
black pepper

a handful of fresh parsley, chopped

boiled rice, to serve

SERVES 4

The bacon adds a special intensity to the flavour of this easy-to-make dish. It crisps up better if dry-fried before adding to the slow cooker as this allows the fat to render out. Serve with rice to mop up the lovely sauce. The dish is already quite salty because of the bacon, so add salt sparingly.

Heat a heavy-based frying pan/skillet until hot then add the bacon and dry-fry for 3–5 minutes, until crisp and golden. Add the mushrooms and cook for 1 further minute. Using a slotted spoon, transfer to a plate.

Add the chicken to the frying pan/skillet and pan-fry for 3–5 minutes, until browned on both sides. Set aside with the bacon.

Heat the olive oil and butter in the frying pan/skillet then fry the garlic and shallots over low heat for 2–3 minutes. Add the flour and mix well then slowly pour in the stock and wine and stir until smooth. Add the bay leaf and season to taste.

Place the chicken breasts in the base of the slow cooker and scatter over the mushrooms and bacon. Pour over the sauce, cover with the lid and cook on HIGH for 3–4 hours. Sprinkle with the chopped parsley and serve with rice.

lemon chicken
with dumplings

4 chicken breasts

2 cloves

1 fresh or dried bay leaf

10 peppercorns

2 celery stalks, halved lengthways
and thinly sliced

½ onion, sliced

1 carrot, halved lengthways and
thinly sliced

150 ml/⅔ cup chicken or vegetable
stock

MARINADE:

grated zest/peel and freshly
squeezed juice of 1 lemon

½ teaspoon salt dissolved in
125 ml/½ cup water

DUMPLINGS:

250 g/2 cups plain/all-purpose flour

1 teaspoon salt

4 teaspoons baking powder

1 tablespoon chopped flat-leaf
parsley (optional)

2 eggs, beaten

2 tablespoons butter, melted

4 tablespoons

SERVES 4

*This is a very simple recipe, so make the most of it
with top-quality free-range chicken. The dumplings
are cooked on top of the casserole so that they
expand and stick together, forming a sort of lid on
top. You can also cook them simply in a saucepan
of boiling salted water.*

Mix the marinade ingredients together in a shallow, non-reactive
dish. Slice each chicken breast into 3 long strips, add to the dish,
cover and chill for 4 hours or overnight.

Place the chicken breasts in the slow cooker and transfer the
marinating liquid to a saucepan. Tie the cloves, bay leaf and
peppercorns in a little cheesecloth bag for easy removal later,
then add to the saucepan. Add the celery, onion, carrot and
chicken stock. Bring to the boil on the stovetop, then transfer to
the slow cooker. Cover with the lid and cook on HIGH for 3–4
hours.

To make the dumplings, sift the flour, salt and baking powder
into a mixing bowl, then stir in the parsley, if using. Make a well
in the centre of the flour, add the eggs, melted butter and milk,
and stir with a fork until a soft ball forms. Do not overwork the
mixture or the dumplings will become heavy when cooked.

Divide the dough into 8 pieces of equal size and roll them into
balls. Place the dumplings on top of the casserole, re-cover with
the lid and cook on HIGH for a further 30 minutes.

coq au vin

6 large skinless chicken breasts

2 tablespoons plain/all-purpose flour, seasoned with salt and pepper plus 1 tablespoon extra for the sauce (optional)

3 tablespoons olive oil

125 g/4 oz. chopped streaky bacon or pancetta cubes

300 g/10 oz. shallots, left whole if small or halved or quartered if larger

2 garlic cloves, thinly sliced

3 tablespoons brandy

3 sprigs of fresh thyme

1 dried bay leaf

1 x 750-ml bottle dry, fruity red wine

250 g/8 oz. small button mushrooms

1 tablespoon butter, softened (optional)

3 tablespoons chopped flat-leaf parsley

sea salt and freshly ground black pepper

creamy mashed potatoes, to serve

SERVES 6

This classic French recipe is a great dish for a slow cooker. Serve with plenty of mashed potatoes.

Dip the chicken breasts in the seasoned flour and coat both sides. Heat 2 tablespoons of the olive oil in a large frying pan/skillet, add the chicken breasts and fry for 2–3 minutes on each side, until lightly browned — you may have to do this in batches.

Remove the chicken from the frying pan/skillet, discard the oil and wipe the pan with a paper towel. Return the frying pan/skillet to the heat and add the remaining oil. Add the bacon and shallots and fry until lightly browned. Stir in the garlic, then return the chicken to the pan. Put the brandy in a small saucepan and heat it until almost boiling. Set it alight with a long kitchen match and carefully pour it over the chicken. Let the flames die down, then add the thyme and bay leaf, and pour in enough wine to cover the chicken. Bring back to simmering point, then transfer to the slow cooker. Cover with the lid and cook on HIGH for 4 hours. After 2 hours, stir in the mushrooms.

If you want to thicken the sauce before serving, remove the chicken from the slow cooker, set aside and keep it warm. Using a slotted spoon, scoop the shallots, bacon pieces and mushrooms out of the slow cooker and keep them warm. Transfer the sauce to a saucepan, increase the heat under the pan and let the sauce simmer until it has reduced by half. Mash 1 tablespoon butter with 1 tablespoon flour to give a smooth roux, then add it bit by bit to the sauce, whisking well after each addition, until the sauce is smooth and glossy. Season to taste.

Cut each chicken breast into 4 slices and arrange them on serving plates. Spoon a generous amount of sauce over the chicken and sprinkle with parsley. Serve with creamy mashed potatoes.

Avgolémono — the liaison of egg yolks and lemon juice stirred into a dish before serving — is one of the hallmarks of Greek cooking. It produces a creamy texture without the heaviness of cream, as well as a refreshing effect which counteracts any richness.

creamy Greek lemon chicken

3 tablespoons butter

2 tablespoons olive oil

1.5-kg/3-lb. chicken, cut into serving pieces, or 1.5-kg/3 lbs. chicken pieces

1 onion, sliced

1 carrot, sliced

1 small celery stalk or slice of fennel, cut into chunks

600 ml/2¼ cups chicken stock

1 tablespoon cornflour/cornstarch

2 egg yolks

2 tablespoons freshly squeezed lemon juice

sea salt and freshly ground black pepper

TO SERVE:

zest/peel of 1 lemon, cut into fine strips or removed with a zester

a few sprigs of fresh dill

SERVES 4

Heat the butter and oil in a large frying pan/skillet. Add the chicken pieces, onion, carrot and celery or fennel and gently fry for about 10–15 minutes, without browning, but turning them over from time to time.

Add the stock and bring to the boil. Transfer to the slow cooker, cover with the lid, and cook on HIGH for 1½ hours.

Turn off the slow cooker and pour off the liquid into a saucepan (keeping the chicken warm in the slow cooker). Bring to the boil and reduce to about 300 ml/1¼ cups. Remove from the heat and let cool for 5 minutes.

Put the cornflour/cornstarch into a cup or small bowl, add 4 tablespoons cold water, and stir until loose. Add the egg yolks, beat well, then beat in 1 tablespoon of the lemon juice. Beat the mixture into the reduced sauce, a little at a time and very slowly. Taste and adjust the seasoning. Add the remaining tablespoon of lemon juice if it needs a little more acidity. Reserve a tablespoon or so of the lemon zest/peel and stir the remainder into the sauce.

Remove the chicken from the slow cooker and pour the sauce over the top. Serve topped with dill and the reserved lemon zest/peel.

chicken tagine with quinces and preserved lemons

1 teaspoon ground saffron

2-cm/1-inch piece of fresh ginger, peeled and grated, or 1 teaspoon ground ginger

1½ tablespoons paprika

1 teaspoon freshly ground black pepper

2 teaspoons ground cinnamon

125 ml/½ cup olive oil

1 chicken, cut into 8 pieces, skinned

2 large onions, grated

a pinch of saffron threads, soaked in boiling water for 30 minutes

6 garlic cloves, crushed

2 cinnamon sticks, broken in half

6 cloves

10 cardamom pods, lightly crushed

2 quinces or slightly unripe pears, cored and cut into wedges

2 preserved lemons (optional)

fresh coriander/cilantro leaves

couscous or rice, to serve

SERVES 4

Tagines often include fruit and quince is a favourite in Morocco but unripe pears can be used instead. Preserved lemons add a salty tang; you can buy them in most larger supermarkets.

Put the ground saffron, ginger, paprika, pepper and ground cinnamon in a bowl and mix well. Rub the chicken pieces in the mixture, put in a bowl, cover with clingfilm/plastic wrap, and marinate for at least 30 minutes or overnight in the refrigerator.

Heat the olive oil in a heavy-based casserole dish. Add the chicken pieces and fry on all sides until golden. Add the onions, then the saffron threads and their soaking liquid, the garlic, cinnamon sticks, cloves and cardamom pods.

Add 125 ml/½ cup cold water and bring to the boil. Transfer to the slow cooker. Cover with the lid and cook on LOW for 4 hours.

Peel the quince wedges, add to the tagine, and continue cooking on LOW for 1 further hour, until the quinces are tender. If using preserved lemons, cut them in quarters and scrape off and discard the flesh. Cut the zest/peel into thick slices lengthways, stir into the tagine, and heat for about 10 minutes. Sprinkle with coriander/cilantro leaves and serve with couscous or rice.

chicken and sweet potatoes with honey, soy and lemon

6 tablespoons/⅓ cup olive oil

2 sweet potatoes, about 1 kg/2 lbs., cut into 1-cm/½-inch rounds

4 skinless chicken legs (thighs and drumsticks)

125 g/1 cup pimento-stuffed green olives

125 ml/½ cup dry white wine

4 tablespoons/¼ cup honey

a large handful of fresh basil leaves

6 garlic cloves, crushed

4 tablespoons/¼ cup light soy sauce

finely grated zest/peel and freshly squeezed juice of 2 lemons

SERVES 4

Sometimes fusions of Western and Eastern ingredients don't work, but this one does, and it's typical of the culinary cross-pollination that happens in Australia and New Zealand. The sweet potato base mops up all the juices from the chicken.

Heat 4 tablespoons/¼ cup of the oil in a large frying pan/skillet. Add the sweet potatoes and fry until lightly browned. Transfer to the slow cooker and arrange in a layer.

Add the remaining oil to the frying pan/skillet, add the chicken and fry until browned all over. Arrange on top of the sweet potatoes.

Put the olives, wine, honey, basil, garlic, soy sauce, lemon zest/peel and juice in a food processor and purée until smooth. Pour this mixture over the chicken and sweet potatoes in the slow cooker. Cover with the lid and cook on HIGH for 3–4 hours.

3 tablespoons vegetable oil

1 onion, roughly chopped

2 garlic cloves, crushed

2 tablespoons hot curry paste

1 tablespoon tomato purée/paste

500 g/1 lb. chicken, cut into bite-size pieces

400 g/14-oz. can chopped tomatoes

1 teaspoon red wine vinegar

100 ml/⅓ cup chicken stock

125 g/4 oz. chargrilled/broiled red (bell) peppers, chopped

125 g/4 oz. courgette/zucchini, diced

sea salt and freshly ground black pepper

fresh coriander/cilantro sprigs, to garnish

TO SERVE

jasmine rice

poppadoms

SERVES 4

chicken jalfrezi

Make sure you have a jar of chargrilled/broiled (bell) peppers for the jalfrezi part and look out for good-quality curry pastes in supermarkets; they cut the time spent grinding or mixing the spices needed for making curry. Go for a hot variety containing spices such as chilli/chile, cumin, coriander, tamarind and turmeric. Serve with jasmine rice and poppadoms.

Heat the oil in a large frying pan/skillet. Add the onion and garlic and fry over medium heat for 5 minutes, until golden. Add the curry paste and tomato purée/paste and cook for 1 minute. Add the chicken and coat well in the spice mixture. Cook for 5 minutes until the chicken is sealed. Transfer to the slow cooker.

Add the chopped tomatoes, vinegar, chicken stock, broiled red (bell) peppers, courgette/zucchini and seasoning to the slow cooker. Cover with the lid and cook on HIGH for 7 hours.

Garnish with the coriander/cilantro and serve with rice and poppadoms.

butter chicken

800 g/1¾ lbs. boneless, skinless chicken, cut into bite-size pieces

3 tablespoons butter

1 large onion, finely chopped

1 cinnamon stick

4 cardamom pods

1 teaspoon mild chilli powder

400 g/14-oz. can chopped tomatoes

100 ml/⅓ cup chicken stock

50 ml/¼ cup single/light cream

salt and freshly ground black pepper

freshly chopped coriander/cilantro, to garnish

basmati rice or naan bread, to serve

MARINADE:

150 g/1 cup cashew nuts

1 tablespoon fennel seeds

2 teaspoons ground cinnamon

1 tablespoon ground coriander

1 teaspoon cardamom seeds, crushed

1 teaspoon black peppercorns

½ teaspoon ground cloves

4 garlic cloves, crushed

2 teaspoons finely grated fresh ginger

2 tablespoons white wine vinegar

6 tablespoons tomato purée/paste

150 g/⅔ cup plain yogurt (not low fat)

SERVES 4

This popular chicken curry is rich and irresistible. Note that the chicken needs to be marinated in the yogurt mixture overnight. Serve with basmati rice or naan bread for a deliciously different dinner.

To make the marinade, heat a nonstick frying pan/skillet and toast the cashew nuts, fennel seeds, cinnamon, coriander, cardamom seeds, peppercorns and cloves for 2–3 minutes, until very aromatic. Transfer to a spice grinder and grind until smooth or grind with a pestle and mortar.

Add this mixture to a food processor with the garlic, ginger, vinegar, tomato purée/paste and yogurt and process until smooth. Transfer to a large glass bowl. Stir in the chicken pieces, cover with clingfilm/plastic wrap and refrigerate overnight.

Melt the butter in a large frying pan/skillet and add the onion, cinnamon stick and cardamom pods. Stir-fry over medium heat for about 6–8 minutes, until the onion has softened. Add the chicken and cook, stirring, for 5 minutes until the chicken is sealed.

Add the chicken mixture to the slow cooker and stir in the chilli powder, canned tomatoes and stock. Cover with the lid and cook on HIGH for 7 hours.

Stir in the cream and coriander/cilantro, season to taste with salt and pepper and serve immediately with rice or naan bread.

The authentic flavour of this curry comes from using fresh spices and the heady, slightly sour taste of bay leaves. Chicken thigh fillets work better here than breast meat as they are harder to over-cook.

chicken and lentil curry with cucumber yogurt

2 tablespoons butter

2 large onions, thinly sliced

2 garlic cloves, peeled and crushed

1½ tablespoons garam masala

500 g/1 lb. chicken thigh fillets or breast fillets, cut into chunks

150 g/⅔ cup passata (Italian strained tomatoes)

8 fresh bay or curry leaves

100 g/⅔ cup red lentils

300 ml/1¼ cups chicken or vegetable stock

sea salt and freshly ground black pepper

fresh coriander/cilantro leaves, to serve

mango chutney and warm chapattis, to serve (optional)

CUCUMBER YOGURT:

150 ml/⅔ cup plain yogurt

¼ cucumber, cut into ribbons with a potato peeler or chopped

SERVES 4

Melt the butter in a large, lidded frying pan/skillet. Add the onions and stir-fry over medium heat. Once they are sizzling, cover with the lid, reduce the heat, and cook for about 2–3 minutes, stirring occasionally. Add the garlic and garam masala. Cook for a further 3–4 minutes, until the spices start to release their aroma and the onions are beginning to turn golden. Remove the onions from the frying pan/skillet and set aside. Add the chicken to the pan and cook for 5–6 minutes, until browned.

Transfer the chicken and onion mixture to the slow cooker and add the passata, bay leaves, lentils and stock. Cover with the lid and cook on HIGH for 3–4 hours.

Meanwhile, to make the cucumber yogurt, put the yogurt in a bowl, add a good pinch of salt and stir in the cucumber.

When the curry is cooked, season it generously (lentils tend to absorb a lot of seasoning so don't be stingy). Transfer to serving bowls, scatter with coriander/cilantro and serve with a dollop of the cucumber yogurt to mix in. Serve with mango chutney and warmed chapattis.

red-cooked chicken legs

150 ml/⅔ cup dark soy sauce

3 tablespoons Chinese rice wine
or dry sherry

2 thin slices of fresh ginger

3 cinnamon sticks, halved

5 whole star anise

2 whole cloves

3 spring onions/scallions

½ teaspoon finely grated orange
or lemon peel

1 tablespoon freshly squeezed
lemon juice

½ teaspoon sugar

4 large chicken legs

rice, noodles or stir-fried vegetables,
to serve

SERVES 4

Chinese red-cooking involves poaching meat, poultry, game or even fish in a dark, soy-based sauce. When the sauce is spiced with star anise, cinnamon and sometimes additional spices from the five-spice brigade, it is used as a 'master sauce'. Master sauce is used like a stock, cooked first as in the recipe below, then stored for later use (you can freeze it). When it has been used a few times, it is considered mature and more desirable. Serve with rice or noodles.

Place the soy sauce and rice wine together in a saucepan, then add the ginger, cinnamon, star anise, cloves, spring onions/scallions, orange or lemon zest/peel, lemon juice and sugar. Bring to the boil and turn off the heat. Leave for at least 10 minutes to infuse the flavours.

Add the chicken legs and bring to the boil. Transfer to the slow cooker, cover with the lid and cook on HIGH for 3–4 hours.

Transfer the chicken to serving plates and spoon over some of the sauce. Serve with rice, noodles or stir-fried vegetables.

chicken, sausage and rice

1 fresh or dried bay leaf

a few sprigs of fresh thyme
and parsley

1 tablespoon olive oil

8 chicken thighs, trimmed

6 pork sausages

1 onion, chopped

1 red (bell) pepper, seeded
and chopped

2 celery stalks, chopped

3 garlic cloves, finely chopped

¼–½ teaspoon dried chilli/hot red
pepper flakes, or more to taste

125 ml/½ cup dry wine, red or white

300 ml/1¼ cups chicken or vegetable
stock

400 g/14-oz. can chopped tomatoes

370 g/2 cups paella rice, or other
short grain rice

200 g/2 cups peas, fresh or frozen
and thawed

sea salt and freshly ground
black pepper

kitchen twine

SERVES 4–6

The ingredients here are of the everyday sort but the inspiration for this recipe came from the Spanish dish paella. You can put it together, put it in the slow cooker and forget about it, almost, until serving time. For some reason the dish tastes better if the ingredients aren't packed in too deeply.

Tie the bay leaf, thyme and parsley together with kitchen twine.

Heat the oil in a large frying pan/skillet. Add the chicken pieces skin-side down and cook on high for 3–5 minutes on each side, until browned. Work in batches if all the pieces will not fit comfortably in the frying pan/skillet. Transfer the browned chicken to a plate and season with salt. Set aside.

Add the sausages to the frying pan/skillet and cook until browned. Remove and cut in 3–4 pieces, depending on their size. Set aside.

Arrange the onion, red (bell) pepper, celery, garlic and chilli/pepper flakes in the slow cooker. Pour in the wine, stock, tomatoes and a pinch of salt and mix well. Add the chicken and sausage and tuck in the herb bundle on the top.

Cover with the lid and cook on HIGH for 3 hours. Add the rice, replace the lid and cook for a further 20 minutes. Put the peas on top and add a little bit of water if the liquid has almost completely evaporated. Cover and cook for a further 10 minutes. Remove the herb bundle and fluff up the rice to mix in the peas. Serve hot.

pancetta and turkey meatballs

500 g/1 lb. ground turkey or chicken

50 g/2 oz. thinly sliced pancetta, coarsely chopped

6 spring onions/scallions, finely chopped

2 garlic cloves, finely chopped

1–2 fresh red chillies/chiles, seeded and finely chopped (optional)

4 tablespoons/¼ cup freshly grated Parmesan cheese, plus extra to serve

1 tablespoon fresh thyme leaves or 1 teaspoon dried thyme

beaten egg, to bind

plain/all-purpose flour, to dust

2 tablespoons olive oil

2 tablespoons/¾ cup red wine

2 x 400 g/14-oz. cans plum tomatoes

1 tablespoon tomato purée/paste

a pinch of sugar

TO SERVE:

300 g/10 oz. dried pasta, such as conchiglie

salt and freshly ground black pepper

SERVES 4

Meatballs are a time-honoured accompaniment to pasta. These delicious little mouthfuls are made with turkey, bacon and herbs, so are somewhat lighter than the traditional all-beef versions.

Put the turkey, pancetta, spring onions/scallions, garlic, chillis/chiles (if using), Parmesan and thyme in a bowl. Add plenty of salt and pepper and just enough beaten egg to bind together then mix well. Using lightly floured hands, shape into 24 small, firm balls then roll each in a little flour to coat.

Heat the oil in a large saucepan. Add the meatballs and cook for about 5 minutes, turning frequently until browned all over. Transfer the meatballs to a plate then add the wine to the saucepan and simmer vigorously for 1–2 minutes to deglaze the pan. Add the tomatoes, breaking them up with a wooden spoon. Stir in the tomato purée/paste, sugar and seasoning to taste. Bring to the boil then pour the sauce into the slow cooker. Add the meatballs, cover with the lid and cook on HIGH for 4 hours.

Meanwhile, bring a large saucepan of water to the boil and cook the pasta according to the packet instructions.

Drain the pasta well and return it to the warm pan. Add the meatballs and sauce to the pasta, toss well to mix then divide between serving bowls. Serve topped with grated Parmesan.

duck casserole with red wine, cinnamon and olives

4 duck legs

2 duck breasts

1 tablespoon olive oil

1 onion, thinly sliced

1 celery stalk, thinly sliced

1 garlic clove, crushed

250 ml/1 cup full-bodied fruity red wine (see recipe introduction), plus 2 tablespoons extra

200 ml/¾ cup passata (Italian strained tomatoes)

2 small strips of orange zest/peel (about 2 cm/1 inch thick)

1 cinnamon stick

100 g/⅔ cup pitted mixed olives (marinated with herbs if available)

½ teaspoon herbes de Provence or dried oregano

sea salt and freshly ground black pepper

rice or couscous, to serve

SERVES 4

Red wine and cinnamon are natural partners and work together brilliantly in this spiced casserole. Use a really strong, fruity wine such as a Merlot or Zinfandel.

Preheat the oven to 200°C(400°F) Gas 6.

Trim any excess fat from the duck legs and prick the skin with a fork. Season all the pieces lightly with salt and pepper. Place on a rack set over an ovenproof dish, skin-side upwards. Roast in the preheated oven for 20–25 minutes, then remove from the oven and pour off the fat (keep it for roasting potatoes.)

Meanwhile, heat the oil in a frying pan/skillet. Add the onion and celery and fry over low heat for 5–6 minutes, until soft. Stir in the garlic, increase the heat and pour in the red wine. Simmer for about 1–2 minutes, then stir in the passata, orange zest/peel, cinnamon, olives and herbs.

Transfer the duck pieces to the slow cooker and spoon the sauce over them. Cook on HIGH for 3½ hours, until the duck is tender. Discard the cinnamon stick and orange zest/peel and spoon off any fat that has accumulated on the surface. Stir in the 2 tablespoons of red wine and season to taste. Serve with rice or couscous.

This is a Creole recipe with the typical trinity of flavourings; garlic, thyme and parsley. The sauce in which the duck cooks has a slightly sweet-sour overtone which cuts the richness of duck.

creole duck

6 duck legs

40 g/¼ cup plain/all-purpose flour

500 ml/2 cups chicken stock

250 ml/1 cup beef stock

3 tablespoons redcurrant jelly

125 ml/½ cup sweet sherry

125 ml/½ cup sherry vinegar

1 tablespoon sugar

2 teaspoons crushed garlic

2 sprigs of fresh thyme

1 tablespoon chopped fresh flat-leaf parsley

sea salt and freshly ground black pepper

braised fennel, to serve (optional)

SERVES 4

Heat a dry, non-stick frying pan/skillet. Working in batches if necessary, add the duck legs and cook over medium heat until well browned. Lots of the fat will run out, so pour it off into a bowl from time to time.

Put the legs in the slow cooker and pour off all but 3 tablespoons of the duck fat in the frying pan/skillet. Add the flour and cook very slowly over medium heat, until the roux is a deep chestnut colour.

Add the stocks and bring to the boil, stirring all the time to make a smooth sauce. Add the redcurrant jelly, sherry, vinegar, sugar, garlic and thyme and continue stirring until the jelly has dissolved.

Add a pinch of salt, then pour the mixture over the duck legs in the slow cooker. Cover with the lid and cook on HIGH for 4 hours. About 30 minutes before the end of cooking time, stir in the chopped parsley. Skim off as much fat as possible, taste and adjust the seasoning before serving with braised fennel, if liked.

bag-cooked chicken
with butter beans

4 skinless chicken breasts

10 baby leeks, washed

100 g/4 oz. baby carrots, halved

400 g/14-oz. can butter beans, drained, rinsed and mashed

100 g/4 oz. baby corn

100 g/4 oz. green beans, trimmed

2–3 garlic cloves, sliced

sprigs of fresh tarragon, plus extra chopped tarragon, to serve

250 ml/1 cup white wine or chicken stock

1 teaspoon Dijon mustard

150 ml/⅔ cup crème fraîche or sour cream

sea salt and freshly ground black pepper

broccoli, to serve (optional)

2 plastic steaming bags

SERVES 4

This is a light and healthy recipe that uses your slow cooker to slowly steam the ingredients in a bag. Use bags made for microwave or conventional ovens, such as steam cooking bags or roasting bags.

Put 2 chicken breasts in each steaming bag and divide the leeks, carrots, butter beans, corn, green beans, garlic, tarragon and white wine between them. Season with salt and pepper and close loosely with a nylon tie and place in the slow cooker. Add enough boiling water to the slow cooker to come about 3–4 cm/1½ inches up the bags. Cover with the lid and cook on HIGH for 1½ hours.

Meanwhile, put the mustard and the crème fraîche in a bowl and mix together. Use tongs to remove the bags from the slow cooker and open carefully. Transfer the contents to serving plates.

Top with a spoonful of the crème fraîche mixture and sprinkle with extra chopped tarragon. Serve immediately on its own or with your choice of green vegetable, such as broccoli.

chicken and barley braise

2 tablespoons wholemeal/whole-wheat flour

500 g/1 lb. skinless chicken breasts, cut into cubes

100 g/4 oz. lean bacon slices, cut into strips

2 onions, chopped

2 carrots, sliced

2 celery stalks, chopped

600 ml/2⅓ cups white wine or chicken stock

3 tablespoons pearl barley, rinsed

1 tablespoon mixed chopped fresh herbs, such as rosemary, basil, parsley and thyme

freshly ground black pepper

chopped fresh parsley

SERVES 4

This is a simple recipe that makes a lighter alternative to a heavy casserole so it's perfect for summer eating. The barley adds a good texture and nutty bite and works very well with the fresh herbs.

Season the flour with black pepper, then toss the chicken cubes in the flour.

Heat a large, nonstick frying pan/skillet or saucepan, add the bacon and dry-fry for 5 minutes, stirring frequently, until the fat starts to run. Add the chicken and fry for 5–8 minutes, turning often, until the chicken is sealed. Remove the chicken and bacon from the pan with a slotted spoon and put in the slow cooker.

Add the onions, carrots, celery and 4 tablespoons of the wine or stock to the pan and fry for 5 minutes, until the vegetables are softened. Add the pearl barley, herbs and the remaining wine or stock. Bring to the boil and pour the mixture over the chicken in the slow cooker. Cover with the lid and cook on HIGH for 3 hours.

Serve sprinkled with chopped parsley and accompanied by a selection of your favourite vegetables.

2 tablespoons safflower or peanut oil

1 tablespoon mustard seeds

2 onions, thinly sliced

2 garlic cloves, crushed

2.5-cm/1-inch piece of fresh ginger, peeled and grated (optional)

a pinch of ground turmeric

4 skinless chicken breasts, cut into 2-cm/¾-inch slices

500 g/1 lb. tomatoes, skinned and roughly chopped

500 g/1 lb. winter squash such a buternut or pumpkin, peeled, seeded, and cut into 1-cm/½-inch cubes

150 ml/⅔ cup double/heavy cream

400 g/14 oz. fresh spinach

1 teaspoon garam masala

sea salt and freshly ground black pepper

basmati rice, to serve

SERVES 4

spicy chicken curry with squash and spinach

Winter squash such as butternut are great for slow cooking as they retain their shape better than other vegetables. This colourful and delicious curry is best served with fluffy steamed basmati rice.

Heat the oil in a large nonstick frying pan/skillet or wok. Add the mustard seeds and fry until they pop. Add the onions and stir-fry gently until softened and translucent. Add the garlic and ginger and stir-fry for 1 minute. Add the turmeric and fry for 1 minute more.

Add the chicken, stir-fry until sealed on all sides, then put in the slow cooker along with the tomatoes and squash. Season generously. Cover with the lid and cook on HIGH for 2½ hours.

Stir in the cream, spinach and garam masala and cook for a further 20–30 minutes. Serve with steamed basmati rice.

fish &

seafood

prawn curry

2 tablespoons vegetable oil

1 onion, finely chopped

3 garlic cloves, crushed

5-cm/2-inch piece of fresh ginger, peeled and finely chopped

1 mild fresh red chilli/chile, seeded and chopped

1 teaspoon ground turmeric

2 teaspoons medium curry powder

1 teaspoon ground coriander

1 teaspoon ground cumin

400-g/14-oz. can chopped tomatoes

100 ml/⅓ cup fish or vegetable stock

freshly squeezed juice of 2 limes

500 g/1 lb. raw tiger/jumbo prawns, thawed if frozen

2 tablespoons chopped fresh coriander/cilantro

sea salt and freshly ground black pepper

basmati rice, to serve

SERVES 4

Tiger/jumbo prawns or extra-large peeled prawns/ shrimp are ideal for this colourful, citrussy curry.

Heat the oil in a large frying pan/skillet. Add the onion, garlic, ginger and chilli/chile and cook for 5 minutes over medium heat.

Add the turmeric, curry powder, ground coriander and cumin and mix well. Transfer to the slow cooker and stir in the tomatoes, stock and lime juice. Cover with the lid and cook on HIGH for 3 hours. Add the prawns/shrimp and cook for a further 1¼ hours. Add the chopped coriander/cilantro and serve with basmati rice.

This is a creamy, garlicky, fish stew from France that's a meal on its own. It is quite different from its sister soup, the bouillabaisse: it is made without tomato, but instead with a rich liaison of egg yolks and mayonnaise beaten in at the end. Traditionally, it would include sea bass, John Dory, whiting, monkfish, sea bream, red gurnard, conger eel and whatever was fresh and firm on the day.

la bourride

1 tablespoon olive oil

1 onion, sliced

1 fennel bulb, sliced

3 garlic cloves, sliced

zest/peel of ½ orange

250 ml/1 cup white wine

800 ml/3 cups hot fish stock

1 bouquet garni

1.5 kg/3 lbs. mixed white fish, cut into large pieces (see recipe introduction)

4 egg yolks

1 garlic clove, crushed

100 ml/⅓ cup olive oil

sea salt and freshly ground black pepper

boiled potatoes or white bread, toasted and cut into triangles, to serve

SERVES 4

Heat the oil in a large saucepan. Add the onion, fennel, garlic and orange zest/peel and fry for 5 minutes without browning.

Add the wine and bring to the boil. Boil until reduced to about 2–3 tablespoons. Transfer to the slow cooker. Add the stock and bouquet garni, then season with salt and plenty of pepper.

Carefully add the pieces of fish, cover with the lid and cook on HIGH for 1½ hours, until the fish is cooked through but remains tender. Carefully remove the fish pieces and keep them warm in a serving dish. Strain the liquid into a large saucepan discarding the vegetables and bouquet garni.

Bring the liquid to the boil and simmer until reduced to about 3 cups. Put the egg yolks and crushed garlic into a small food processor or bowl, then gradually work in the olive oil, drop by drop, to form a thick mayonnaise. Gradually whisk the mixture into the fish stock. Still stirring, bring the mixture almost to the boil (do not let it reach the boil, or the eggs will scramble.)

Remove from the heat, then strain the sauce back over the fish in the serving dish. Serve with boiled potatoes or the traditional accompaniment of crisp toast.

Mediterranean chunky fish stew with cheese toasts

1 tablespoon olive oil

1 small onion, finely chopped

2 garlic cloves; 1 crushed, 1 peeled and halved

a pinch of dried thyme

125 g/5 oz. fennel, cored and finely chopped

50 ml/¼ cup Noilly Prat, dry Martini, or dry white wine

300 ml/1¼ cups passata (Italian sieved tomatoes)

a pinch of saffron threads

freshly squeezed juice and grated zest/peel of 1 orange

200 g/7 oz. skinless cod fillet, cut into large chunks

4 thin slices of baguette

50 g/1 cup finely grated Emmental or Gruyère cheese

sea salt and freshly ground black pepper

SERVES 2

If you have ever tasted the classic French fish soup bouillabaisse and enjoyed the flavour, then this is a good slow cooker version. The combination of saffron, orange and fennel gives the stew its distinctive flavour. If you can't find Noilly Prat, use dry Martini or a dry white wine in its place.

Heat the oil in a large saucepan. Add the onion, crushed garlic, thyme and fennel and gently fry for about 6–8 minutes, until soft. Add the Noilly Prat and let bubble, uncovered, until the liquid has almost reduced to nothing.

Add the passata, saffron, orange juice and zest/peel, and 150 ml/⅔ cup cold water. Increase the heat. Add the cod fillet and bring to the boil. Transfer to the slow cooker, season to taste and cook on LOW for 2–2½ hours.

Meanwhile, preheat the grill/broiler to high. Toast the baguette slices on each side under the grill/broiler until lightly golden. Rub the halved garlic over each slice and sprinkle with the grated cheese.

Ladle the stew into warmed deep serving bowls and balance the cheese-topped toasts on top. Serve immediately.

shellfish, tomato and couscous stew

2 tablespoons light olive oil

1 red onion, chopped

1 garlic clove, chopped

1 small red (bell) pepper, seeded and thinly sliced

750 ml/3 cups chicken stock

2 tomatoes, chopped

3 heaped tablespoons couscous

10–12 saffron threads

300 g/10 oz. any firm white fish fillet, cut into bite-size cubes

12 mussels, scrubbed and cleaned of beards

12 raw prawns/jumbo shrimp, shelled and deveined

4 small squids, hoods cut into 1-cm/½-inch wide pieces (optional)

1 large handful of fresh parsley, roughly chopped

sea salt and freshly ground black pepper

lemon wedges, to serve (optional)

SERVES 4

This is a very simple and tasty summer dish featuring ripe tomatoes with a combination of really fresh seafood. Once you become more familiar with the recipe you can add any combination of your favourite seafood — pieces of salmon fillet (replacing the white fish) would work very well. Couscous shows its versatility in this recipe too, acting as a thickener, like rice, barley or pasta.

Heat the olive oil in a saucepan set over high heat. Add the onion, garlic and (bell) pepper and cook for 4–5 minutes, until softened.

Add the stock, tomatoes, couscous and saffron to the pan and bring to the boil. Season lightly. Add the white fish and mussels. Transfer to the slow cooker. Cover with the lid and cook on LOW for 1½ hours then add the prawns/shrimp and squid (if using) and cook on LOW for a further 30 minutes. (If using squid do not cook for longer than 30 minutes as overcooking it will make it very tough.)

Serve in bowls with the parsley scattered over the top and the lemon wedges on the side to squeeze over, if using.

This makes a great light dish. The creamy butter beans work surprisingly well with the prawns/shrimp. Feel free to add additional vegetables of your choice. Peas, green beans or sweetcorn/corn kernels all make a good addition, however adding frozen food to a slow cooker isn't recommended so if using frozen, defrost first.

prawn and butter bean rice

1 large onion, chopped

1 teaspoon ground turmeric

400-g/14-oz. can chopped tomatoes

1 large red (bell) pepper, seeded and finely chopped

1–2 garlic cloves, chopped

500 ml/2 cups fish or vegetable stock

200 g/1 cup basmati rice

400-g/14-oz. can butter beans, drained and rinsed

1–2 fresh red chillies/chiles, seeded and thinly sliced

500 g/1 lb. cooked peeled prawns/shrimp, thawed if frozen

3 tablespoons fresh coriander/cilantro, coarsely chopped

sea salt and freshly ground black pepper

SERVES 4

Put the onion, turmeric, tomatoes, (bell) pepper, garlic and stock in the slow cooker. Cover with the lid and cook on HIGH for 3 hours, until the vegetables are tender.

Add the rice, butter beans and chillies/chiles and stir through gently. Replace the lid and cook for a further 30 minutes. Stir in the prawns/shrimp, replace the lid and cook for another 10 minutes, until the stock is absorbed and the prawns/shrimp are warmed through. Season to taste. Stir in the coriander/cilantro and serve immediately.

Tip

For a speedier preparation time, pour a jar of prepared marinara sauce, 1 teaspoon ground turmeric, and 500 ml/2 cups fish or vegetable stock into the slow cooker. Cover with the lid and cook on high for 2 hours. Add the rice, butter beans, prawns/shrimp, chilli/chile, seasoning and coriander/cilantro as directed above.

900 g/2 lbs. skinless chunky fresh fish fillets, such as cod or haddock, cut into large chunks

2–3 tablespoons olive oil

1 red onion, finely chopped

2 carrots, finely chopped

2 celery stalks, finely chopped

1 preserved lemon, pips discarded and flesh finely chopped

400-g/14-oz. can plum tomatoes with their juice

150 ml/⅔ cup fish stock or water

150 ml/⅔ cup white wine or fino sherry

sea salt and freshly ground black pepper

a bunch of fresh mint leaves, finely shredded

new potatoes and salad greens, to serve (optional)

CHERMOULA:

2–3 garlic cloves, chopped

1 fresh red chilli/chile, seeded and chopped

1 teaspoon sea salt

a small bunch of fresh coriander/cilantro, roughly chopped

a pinch of saffron threads

2 teaspoons ground cumin

3–4 tablespoons olive oil

freshly squeezed juice of 1 lemon

SERVES 4–6

The fish stews of coastal Morocco are often made with whole fish, or with large chunks of fleshy fish such as sea bass, monkfish and cod. The fish is first marinated in the classic chermoula flavouring, and this tasty dish is given an additional fillip with a little white wine or sherry. Serve with new potatoes and leafy salad greens, if liked.

Moroccan fish stew with mint

First, make the chermoula. Simply whizz all the ingredients together in a blender or small food processor. Reserve about 2 teaspoons of the mixture for cooking. Toss the fish chunks in the remaining chermoula, cover, and let marinate in the fridge for 1–2 hours.

Heat the oil in a frying pan/skillet. Add the onion, carrots, and celery and fry for 2–3 minutes, until softened. Add the preserved lemon (reserving a little for sprinkling) with the reserved 2 teaspoons of chermoula and the tomatoes and stir in well. Cook gently for about 5 minutes to reduce the liquid slightly, then add the stock and the wine. Bring the liquid to the boil then transfer to the slow cooker. Stir the marinated fish and marinade into the sauce, cover with the lid, and cook on HIGH for 3 hours.

Season to taste, sprinkle with the reserved preserved lemon and the shredded mint leaves, and serve immediately with potatoes and salad greens, if liked.

vegetarian
dishes

potato, basil and green bean risotto

4 new potatoes, scrubbed and cut into 1-cm/½-inch cubes

50 g/2 oz. green beans, cut into ½-inch lengths

3¼ cups hot vegetable stock

50 g/3 tablespoons unsalted butter

1 tablespoon olive oil

6–8 shallots depending on size, finely chopped

2 garlic cloves, crushed

275 g/1½ cups risotto rice, such as arborio

75 ml/⅓ cup white wine

100 g/1½ cups freshly grated Parmesan cheese

a large handful of fresh basil, leaves torn

sea salt and freshly ground black pepper

TO SERVE:

fresh basil leaves

extra virgin olive oil (optional)

fresh pesto (optional)

SERVES 4

At first you might be alarmed at the combination of potatoes, rice and beans. Don't be, because it's absolutely delicious and makes a substantial meal. Spooning fresh pesto on top before serving is optional, but if you love basil, this will intensify the flavour dramatically.

Put the potatoes and beans in the slow cooker with 1⅔ cups of hot stock. Cover with the lid and cook on HIGH for 2 hours. About 15 minutes before the end of cooking time, heat the butter and oil in a saucepan set over medium heat. Add the shallots and cook for 1–2 minutes, until softened but not browned. Add the garlic and mix well.

Add the rice to the pan and stir, using a wooden spoon, for about 1 minute, until the grains are well coated and glistening. Pour in the wine and stir until it has been completely absorbed.

Transfer to the slow cooker and stir into the potato and bean mixture along with the remaining hot stock. Cover with the lid and cook on HIGH for 1 further hour. The risotto is ready when the liquid has been absorbed and the rice is tender but still firm (al dente). Turn off the slow cooker, cover with the lid, and let rest for 3–4 minutes.

Add the Parmesan and basil and season to taste. Mix well. Spoon into serving bowls, top with basil leaves and drizzle with olive oil or fresh pesto, if using. Serve immediately.

risotto with cannellini beans

Cannellini beans with pasta or rice make a much-loved meal in Italy. Other beans, such as borlotti or flageolets, are also delicious. Use arborio risotto rice in this dish as it will give a creamy texture.

900 ml/3⅔ cups hot vegetable stock

50 g/3 tablespoons unsalted butter

2 tablespoons olive oil

8 shallots, finely chopped

2 garlic cloves, crushed

275 g/1½ cups risotto rice, such as arborio

75 ml/⅓ cup white wine

250 g/1¼ cups canned cannellini beans, rinsed and drained

4 firm tomatoes, seeded and chopped

finely grated zest/peel of 1 lemon

100 g/1½ cups freshly grated Parmesan cheese

a handful of fresh basil leaves, torn or finely chopped rosemary

a handful of fresh flat-leaf parsley, finely chopped

sea salt and freshly ground black pepper

extra virgin olive oil, to serve (optional)

SERVES 4

Heat the butter and 1 tablespoon of the oil in a sauté pan set over medium heat. Add the shallots and cook for 1–2 minutes, until softened but not browned. Add the garlic and mix well.

Add the rice and stir, using a wooden spoon, for about 1 minute, until the grains are well coated and glistening. Pour in the wine and stir until it has been completely absorbed.

Add 1 ladle of hot stock and simmer, stirring until it has been absorbed. After 10 minutes, add the cannellini beans, tomatoes and lemon zest/peel and mix well. Transfer the ingredients to the slow cooker and add more hot stock to make up to 700 ml/2¾ cups altogether. Cover with the lid and cook on HIGH for 1 hour. After 1 hour, stir well, add the remaining hot stock, replace the lid and cook for a further 30 minutes. The risotto is ready when the liquid has been absorbed and the rice is tender but still firm (al dente). Turn off the slow cooker, cover and let rest for 3–4 minutes.

Add the Parmesan and half of the herbs and season to taste. Spoon into warmed serving bowls, sprinkle with the remaining herbs and drizzle with olive oil, if using. Serve immediately.

The lemon adds a delicious lightness of flavour to this unusual risotto. Do use a good risotto rice such as arborio or carnaroli. Beating the risotto at the end of cooking gives this dish its lovely creamy quality. Serve it with plenty of freshly grated Parmesan cheese to sprinkle on top.

lemon, fennel and mushroom risotto

2 tablespoons olive oil

50 g/3 tablespoons unsalted butter

1 onion, finely chopped

1 fennel bulb, trimmed and chopped, feathery tops reserved

350 g/1½ cups risotto rice

1.25 litres/5 cups hot vegetable stock

coarsely grated zest/peel and freshly squeezed juice of 1 lemon

1 small fresh or dried bay leaf

a few sprigs of fresh tarragon

250 g/8 oz. button mushrooms, sliced

125 g/½ cup mascarpone cheese

75 g/¾ cup freshly grated Parmesan cheese

sea salt and freshly ground black pepper

SERVES 4–5

Put half of the oil and half of the butter in a deep frying pan/skillet or saucepan and heat until melted. Add the onion, fennel and a pinch of salt and cook very gently for about 10 minutes, until soft and golden but not browned. Add the rice, stir around in the buttery juices and cook over medium heat for 2–3 minutes, until the rice looks translucent.

Transfer to the slow cooker and add about 750 ml/3 cups of the hot stock, ½ teaspoon salt, half of the lemon zest/peel, the bay leaf and tarragon. Mix together, cover with the lid and cook on HIGH for 1 hour, then stir in the remaining stock and cook for a further 25–30 minutes. The risotto is ready when the liquid has been absorbed and the rice is tender but still firm (al dente).

Meanwhile, heat the remaining butter and oil in a frying pan/skillet and cook the mushrooms over medium heat, until tender but not browned. Increase the heat and squeeze in half of the lemon juice. Let the liquid evaporate, then take the mushrooms off the heat.

As soon as the rice is cooked, beat in the mascarpone, most of the remaining lemon juice and half the Parmesan. Stir in the mushrooms and season to taste. Turn off the slow cooker, cover and let rest for 3–4 minutes. Stir well and serve in warmed serving bowls, sprinkled with the chopped fennel tops and the remaining lemon zest/peel. Serve with the remaining Parmesan.

Many exotic mushroom varieties are now cultivated and can be bought year-round, offering a constant supply of just about any mushroom you could wish for. A mixture has been used here, including meaty field mushrooms as they go hand in hand with the other comforting, rich flavours of fresh thyme, red wine and cinnamon.

2 tablespoons olive oil

2 tablespoons unsalted butter

1 onion, chopped

2 garlic cloves, chopped

3 portobello mushrooms, caps removed and cut into 2-cm/1-inch pieces

200 g/6 oz. button mushrooms

100 g/3 oz. shiitake mushrooms, quartered

3 fresh thyme sprigs

200 ml/¾ cup red wine

1 cinnamon stick

100 ml/⅓ cup vegetable stock

400 g/14 oz. fresh lasagne sheets, cut or torn into thick strips

sea salt and freshly ground black pepper

freshly grated Parmesan cheese, to serve

SERVES 4

mushroom and thyme ragù with hand-torn pasta

Heat the oil and butter in a heavy-based saucepan set over medium heat. Add the onion and garlic and cook for 4–5 minutes, until the onions have softened.

Increase the heat, add the mushrooms and thyme and cook for a further 8–10 minutes, stirring often, until the mushrooms darken and soften.

Add the red wine and cinnamon to the pan and boil for 5 minutes. Pour in the stock and season well. Transfer everything to the slow cooker, cover with the lid and cook on HIGH for 2 hours.

Cook the pasta in a saucepan of boiling water for 2–3 minutes, until it rises to the surface. Drain well and put in warmed serving bowls. Spoon the mushroom ragù on top and sprinkle with Parmesan to serve.

3 tablespoons olive oil

1 onion, chopped

2 garlic cloves, chopped

½ teaspoon ground turmeric

½ teaspoon paprika

1 teaspoon ground cumin

1 cinnamon stick

300 ml/1¼ cups vegetable stock

400-g/14-oz. can chopped tomatoes

1 large carrot, peeled and cut into
thick batons

1 parsnip, peeled and cut into
2–3-cm/1-inch pieces

1 turnip, peeled and cut into 1-cm/
½-inch thick rounds

125 g/4 oz. sweet potato, peeled and
cut into cubes

1 green apple, peeled, cored and
cut into 8 wedges

a small handful of fresh mint
leaves, roughly chopped

sea salt and freshly ground
black pepper

couscous or rice, to serve

SERVES 4

Although it sounds rather exotic, a tagine is really nothing more complicated than a stew. It really can have just about anything you like in it, provided there are the obligatory fragrant and aromatic spices, so typical of Moroccan cooking. It's these heavy, pungent spices that work so well here with full-flavoured winter vegetables.

winter vegetable tagine

Heat the oil in a heavy-based saucepan. Add the onion and garlic and cook over high heat for 2–3 minutes. Add all of the spices and cook for 2 minutes more, until aromatic but not burning.

Add the stock and the tomatoes and season well. Bring to the boil and add the carrot, parsnip, turnip, sweet potato and apple. Transfer to the slow cooker, cover with the lid, and cook on HIGH for 3 hours.

Stir in the mint then spoon the vegetables over couscous or rice to serve.

2 tablespoons olive oil

1 large onion, chopped

2 garlic cloves, chopped

1 tablespoon capers, finely chopped

3 tablespoons chopped fresh
flat-leaf parsley

2 teaspoons smoked sweet Spanish
paprika (pimentón dulce)

1 celery stalk, chopped

1 carrot, chopped

2 medium waxy potatoes, cut into
2-cm/1-inch dice

1 red (bell) pepper, seeded and
chopped

350 ml/1⅓ cups hot vegetable stock

400-g/14-oz. can butter/lima beans

sea salt and freshly ground
black pepper

crusty bread, to serve

SERVES 4

*This is a hearty and filling bean hotpot packed with
vegetables and rich with smoky Spanish paprika.*

smoky bean hotpot

Put the oil in a saucepan set over medium heat. Add the onion
and cook for 4–5 minutes, until softened. Add the garlic, capers,
parsley and paprika to the pan and stir-fry for 2 minutes.

Add the celery, carrot, potatoes and red (bell) pepper and cook
for 2 minutes, stirring constantly to coat the vegetables in the
flavoured oil. Transfer to the slow cooker and add the stock.

Cover with the lid and cook on HIGH for 3 hours, until all the
vegetables are cooked. Stir in the butter/lima beans 1 hour
before the end of cooking time.

Season to taste and serve with crusty bread.

maple baked beans

2 tablespoons olive oil

3 garlic cloves, chopped

1 large onion, chopped

1 red (bell) pepper, seeded and diced

250 ml/1 cup good-quality barbecue sauce

2 tablespoons yellow American mustard

2 tablespoons cider vinegar

2 x 400-g/14-oz. cans borlotti or pinto beans, drained

60 ml/¼ cup pure maple syrup

6 bacon slices (optional)

sea salt and freshly ground black pepper

SERVES 4

Known as 'brown bellies' in diners, these delicious baked beans are traditionally served as a side dish to barbecued ribs or pulled pork sandwiches. Although this recipe contains optional bacon, they are also unashamedly good eaten on toast or with vegetarian sausages as a meat-free main dish.

Put the olive oil in a frying pan/skillet and set over medium heat. Add the garlic, onion and red (bell) pepper and fry for 5 minutes, just until softened.

Add the barbecue sauce, 50 ml/¼ cup water, the mustard, vinegar, beans and maple syrup. Transfer to the slow cooker and then lay the bacon slices over everything (if using).

Cover with the lid and cook on HIGH for 4 hours. To serve break up the bacon into bite-size pieces.

Macaroni cheese is a firm comfort food favourite. Here it's given a modern makeover with upmarket cheeses like mascarpone and Parmesan and a touch of garlic. If you like a crisp topping, you can simply pop the slow cooker dish under a preheated grill/ broiler to brown for a few minutes before serving.

three-cheese macaroni

2 tablespoons butter

1 garlic clove, finely chopped

1 teaspoon dry mustard powder

3 tablespoons all-purpose flour

600 ml/2⅓ cups milk

125 ml/½ cup mascarpone cheese

130 g/1 cup grated mature/sharp Cheddar cheese

60 g/½ cup grated Parmesan cheese

250 g/8 oz. dried tube pasta, such as macaroni, penne or rigatoni

toasted breadcrumbs, to serve

sea salt and freshly ground black pepper

SERVES 4

Melt the butter in a medium saucepan and use some to brush the inside of the slow cooker dish. Add the garlic and mustard to the pan and fry for 1 minute before adding the flour. Whisk constantly over medium heat until it forms a paste. Gradually whisk in the milk and increase the heat. Bring to the boil, whisking constantly. Remove from the heat and stir in the mascarpone, Cheddar and half of the Parmesan.

Boil the pasta in plenty of salted water until just al dente. Drain and mix with the cheese sauce. Season to taste and spoon the mixture into the slow cooker. Top with the remaining Parmesan. Cover with the lid and cook on LOW for 2–3 hours. Sprinkle with the toasted breadcrumbs to serve.

root vegetable ragù

3 tablespoons olive oil

2 tablespoons unsalted butter

1 red onion, chopped

1 celery stalk, roughly chopped

6 garlic cloves, lightly smashed

250 ml/1 cup passata (Italian sieved tomatoes)

250 ml/1 cup vegetable stock

2 tablespoons fresh oregano leaves or 1 teaspoon dried oregano

1 parsnip, diced

2 carrots, diced

6 small, waxy, new potatoes, diced

sea salt and freshly ground black pepper

couscous or rice, to serve

SERVES 4

This is a hearty dish packed with nutritious root vegetables — perfect comfort food for vegetarians.

Put the oil and butter in a large frying pan/skillet set over medium heat. When the butter sizzles, add the onion, celery and garlic. Cook for 1–2 minutes, then add the remaining ingredients, season to taste and bring to the boil.

Transfer to the slow cooker, cover with the lid and cook on HIGH for 2–3 hours, until the vegetables are tender.

Spoon the ragù over couscous or rice to serve.

butternut and courgette pulao

125 ml/½ cup safflower oil

2 cloves, crushed

1 teaspoon cumin seeds

1 onion, finely sliced

½ teaspoon ground turmeric

1 tablespoon cardamom pods, crushed

1 cinnamon stick, broken

2 fresh bay leaves

½ cauliflower head, separated into florets

½ butternut squash, peeled, seeded and cut into small cubes

2 potatoes, cut into small cubes

1 carrot, cut into small cubes

2-cm/1-inch piece of fresh ginger, peeled and grated

a pinch of sugar

200 g/1 cup peas

500 g/2 cups basmati rice, washed and drained

4 courgettes/zucchini, cut into small chunks

TO SERVE:

2 pinches of saffron threads

100 g/⅔ cup cashew nuts

100 g/⅔ cup shelled pistachios

a large handful of fresh coriander/cilantro leaves (optional)

SERVES 8–10

Pulaos were born in Persia, but versions are found all the way from India to the Middle East and Spain. The name changes from pulao to pullaw, pilaf and then paella along the way. Use aromatic basmati rice for this dish.

Heat 5 tablespoons of the safflower oil in a large, heavy-based saucepan. Add the cloves and cumin seeds and fry for about 10 seconds. Add the onion and turmeric and stir-fry until softened and translucent. Add the cardamom, cinnamon, bay leaves, cauliflower, butternut, potatoes and carrot. Stir-fry until covered with oil, then transfer to the slow cooker. Add 4 cups cold water, the ginger, and sugar.

Cover with the lid and cook on HIGH for 2 hours, until the vegetables are starting to soften. Stir in the peas and rice so that the rice is completely submerged by the liquid. Cover with the lid and cook for another 30 minutes, until all the water has been absorbed and the rice is fluffy. (Do not lift the lid, or you will spoil it.)

Meanwhile, heat the remaining oil in a small frying pan/skillet, add the courgettes/zucchini and stir-fry for 1–2 minutes at high heat, until lightly browned but still firm. Set aside. Soak the saffron threads in a couple of tablespoons of hot water.

Turn out the rice onto a serving dish, remove the bay leaves, add the courgettes/zucchini, then carefully drizzle over the saffron liquid to make yellow trails in the rice. Sprinkle with the cashew and pistachio nuts and the coriander/cilantro. Serve immediately.

Choose small sugar pumpkins or butternut squash for this recipe (just the bottom half and use the top piece for other recipes). This is marvellous served with salad as a vegetarian main course.

stuffed squash with pesto and mozzarella

2 small butternut squash or 4 sugar pumpkins, washed and dried

1 tablespoon olive oil, plus extra to drizzle

½ small red onion, diced

1 garlic clove, crushed

8 cherry tomatoes, halved

a large handful of fresh basil leaves

2 tablespoons fresh pesto

75 g/2½ oz. mozzarella cheese, torn into pieces

sea salt and freshly ground black pepper

crisp, peppery salad greens, to serve (optional)

SERVES 2

Cut the butternut squash just as they start to narrow into a waist and scoop out the seeds. You're aiming for a hollow receptacle. Save the tops for another recipe. (If using sugar pumpkins or small squash, simply slice off the tops and reserve these for decoration.) Arrange the squash in the base of the slow cooker, trimming off any end parts to make them fit if slightly too big.

Heat the oil in a frying pan/skillet, add the onion and garlic and fry for 2–3 minutes, until softened. Remove from the heat and stir in the tomatoes, basil, pesto and mozzarella. Season well then divide the filling between the squash. Drizzle a little olive oil over the top and then very carefully pour in enough water to come just under halfway up the sides of the squash. You do not want to spill any water on or in the squash or to allow the filling of the squash to come into contact with the water.

Cover with the lid and cook on HIGH for 3 hours, until the squash is tender. Serve hot with crisp, peppery salad greens, if liked.

ratatouille

3 tablespoons olive oil

1 onion, finely sliced

3 garlic cloves, crushed

a small bunch of fresh flat-leaf parsley, chopped

1 large aubergine/eggplant, cubed

2–3 red and/or yellow (bell) peppers, seeded and cubed

4 medium courgette/zucchini, sliced

¼ teaspoon sea salt

400-g/14-oz. can chopped tomatoes in rich juice

2 teaspoons red wine vinegar or balsamic vinegar

sea salt and freshly ground black pepper

rice or crusty bread, to serve

SERVES 6

Ratatouille is simply the best all-purpose vegetable dish there is. It goes perfectly with any main dish or served with rice or crusty bread for a vegetarian meal. It also makes a great filling for a savoury pancake when sprinkled with cheese and finished off under the grill/broiler.

Heat the oil in a large, heavy-based saucepan set over medium heat. Add the onion, garlic and parsley and fry for 10 minutes, stirring regularly.

Add the aubergine/eggplant and cook for 5 minutes. Add the (bell) peppers and courgettes/zucchini and stir in the salt. Cook for a few minutes, then add the chopped tomatoes.

Transfer to the slow cooker, cover with the lid, and cook on HIGH for 3½ hours. About 1 hour before the end of the cooking time, stir in the vinegar and season to taste. Serve warm with rice or bread.

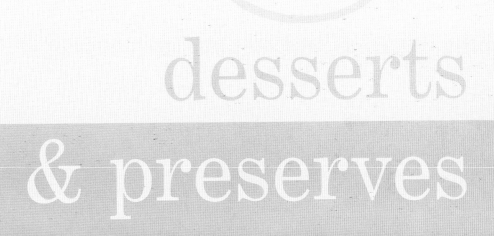

desserts
& preserves

peaches poached in vanilla honey syrup

2 tablespoons honey

1 vanilla pod/bean, split lengthways

4 peaches, firm, unpeeled, pitted and halved

125 g/1 cup fresh raspberries

vanilla ice cream, to serve (optional)

SERVES 4

This is such a delicious dessert that you feel it must be bad for you. In fact, fresh fruit and fragrant honey are all that are needed to make this so good, so why not treat yourself to a large scoop of vanilla ice cream on the side!

Put 250 ml/1 cup water, the honey and vanilla pod/bean in a large saucepan. Bring to the boil over high heat, then reduce the heat, cover, and simmer gently for 5 minutes to let the vanilla impart its flavour.

Put the prepared peaches in the slow cooker. Pour over the hot syrup, cover with the lid and cook on HIGH for about 3 hours, until the peaches are tender. (Time will vary according to size and ripeness of fruit.) Remove the peaches from the pan with a slotted spoon.

While the peaches cool for a few minutes, transfer the syrup to a saucepan and boil until it reduces by about half.

When the peaches are cool enough to handle, peel off their skins, which should come off like little jackets. Serve a couple of peach halves in a bowl with some raspberries and drizzle with the syrup. Serve with a large scoop of vanilla ice cream, if liked.

This lovely, fruity dessert is good for you as well as delicious. If blackberries are not available, use blueberries instead.

baked apples with blackberries and port sauce

4 cooking apples, rinsed and cored

1 tablespoon freshly squeezed lemon juice

50 g/½ cup blackberries, thawed if frozen

1 tablespoon slivered almonds

½ teaspoon ground allspice

½ teaspoon finely grated lemon zest/peel

300 ml/1¼ cups ruby port

4 tablespoons honey

1 cinnamon stick, bruised

2 teaspoons cornflour/cornstarch

cream, to serve (optional)

SERVES 4

Make a shallow cut through the skin around the middle of each apple with a small, sharp knife — this will help the apples to cook. Brush the centres of the cored apples with the lemon juice to prevent them browning.

Put the blackberries, almonds, allspice and lemon zest/peel in a bowl and mix. Using a teaspoon, spoon the mixture into the centre of each apple. Place the stuffed apples in the slow cooker, pour the port around the apples and drizzle the honey over the fruit. Add the cinnamon stick and cover with the lid. Cook on HIGH for 1½ hours.

Turn the slow cooker off and drain the cooking juices through a sieve/ strainer into a saucepan, discarding the cinnamon stick. (Keep the apples warm in the slow cooker.) Bring the juice to the boil. Put the cornflour/cornstarch in a small bowl and blend to a smooth paste with 1 tablespoon of water. Add the paste to the boiling liquid and cook, stirring, until thickened.

Transfer the apples to warmed serving plates and pour over the port sauce. Serve immediately with cream, if liked.

Muscat is a grape variety that produces deliciously sweet and syrupy dessert wines known as moscato in Italy and moscatel in Spain. Whichever one you choose, the result will be the same — a deliciously fragrant and light dessert that will wow your guests.

spiced muscat figs

350 ml/1½ cups muscat (or other sweet dessert wine)

125 g/½ cup sugar

1 vanilla pod/bean, split lengthways

2 cardamom pods, lightly crushed

2 strips of orange zest/peel

8 fresh green figs

SERVES 4

Put the wine, sugar, vanilla, cardamom pods and orange zest/peel in a medium saucepan set over high heat. Bring the mixture to the boil, then transfer to the slow cooker.

Add the figs, cover with the lid and cook on HIGH for 1½ hours, until the figs are very tender.

Transfer the figs to warmed serving bowls and serve immediately with the syrup spooned over the top.

125 g/1 cup self-raising/rising flour

1½ teaspoons baking powder

a pinch of salt

125 g/½ cup sugar

finely grated zest/peel of 2 lemons

2 eggs, beaten

125 g/1 stick unsalted butter, melted,
then cooled

3 drops of lemon oil

50 ml/¼ cup milk mixed with 50 ml/
¼ cup cold water

LEMON BUTTER SAUCE:

6 tablespoons sugar

finely grated zest/peel and freshly
squeezed juice of 2 lemons, plus
the freshly squeezed juice of
1 extra lemon

2 tablespoons Cointreau or other
orange-flavoured liqueur

100 g/1 stick unsalted butter, chilled
and cubed

4 individual pudding pans or a
1.5-litre/1½-quart ceramic bowl,
greased, then dredged with a
mixture of flour and sugar

SERVES 4

baked lemon dessert with lemon butter sauce

A very light, fresh, and lemony dessert with a zingy
lemon sauce — and it couldn't be simpler to make.

To make the sponge, sift the flour, baking powder, salt and sugar
into a bowl and stir in the grated zest/peel. Make a well in the
centre and add the eggs, butter, lemon oil and milk mixture.
Mix with a small whisk to form a smooth batter.

Pour into the prepared pans or bowl then cover each loosely
with foil and place in the slow cooker. Add enough water to come
halfway up the dishes. Cover and cook the individual desserts
on HIGH for 1½ hours or the large one for 3–3½ hours, until well
risen and springy. The sponges should feel as firm in the middle
as they do at the sides. Turn the pans upside down onto a wire
rack and let cool for 5 minutes. Ease a small knife around the
side of the pans to loosen, then gently shake out.

To make the sauce, put the sugar and lemon juice into a small,
non-reactive saucepan and dissolve gently over low heat. Add
the lemon zest/peel and bring to the boil. Cook at a fast bubble for
2–3 minutes to reduce the liquid to a thick syrup. Remove from
the heat and strain out the zest/peel. Add the Cointreau, then
whisk in the chilled butter, a little at a time, until the sauce is
thickened and glossy.

Serve with the sauce poured over and around each dessert.

blueberry and cherry sponge

500 g/1 lb. mixed red fruit such as cherries and blueberries, pitted

125 g/¾ cup sugar, plus 3 extra tablespoons

125 g/1 cup self-raising/rising flour

a pinch of salt

1 teaspoon baking powder

125 g/1 stick unsalted butter, softened

2 UK large/US extra-large eggs, lightly beaten

finely grated zest/peel of 1 orange

crème anglaise or cream, to serve

1.2-litre/1-quart ceramic bowl, greased, then dredged with a mixture of flour and sugar

SERVES 4–6

This is a deliciously moist and fruity steamed sponge — the perfect end to any family meal.

Reserve 125 g/5 oz. of the fruit and 1 tablespoon of the sugar. Mix the remaining fruit with 2 tablespoons of the sugar, then transfer to the prepared bowl. Sift the flour, salt and baking powder into a second bowl.

Put the softened butter and remaining 125 g/¾ cup sugar in a mixing bowl and beat until very light, fluffy and creamy in colour. Add the eggs, a little at a time, beating between each addition, until the mixture is light and fluffy. Add the orange zest/peel.

Sift half the flour mixture over the butter mixture and lightly fold in the flour with a metal spoon. Repeat with the remaining flour, taking care not to over-mix: the mixture should drop softly off the spoon. If it is too stiff, fold in about 1 tablespoon of water to make a soft dropping consistency. Spoon the mixture over the fruit in the bowl, starting at the edges and working towards the centre. Level the top, making a slight indentation with the spoon in the middle.

Cover loosely with a layer of baking parchment. Fold a sheet of foil down the middle to make a pleat — this will allow for expansion. Put on top of the bowl and tie a length of kitchen twine firmly around the edge, under the lip of the basin. Tie a handle of string from side to side. Use this handle to lower the bowl into the slow cooker. Add enough boiling water to come two thirds of the way up the basin. Cook on HIGH for 5 hours, until golden, well risen, and as firm in the middle as it is at the sides. Let settle before turning out onto a serving dish.

To make the sauce, put the reserved fruit and sugar in a blender and blend to a smooth purée. Serve the sponge with the fruit sauce and cream or custard sauce, as preferred.

Served with a sharp, fresh apricot and brandy sauce, this homely dessert becomes an altogether more elegant dish, fit for a dinner party.

apricot bread and butter pudding

450 ml/1¾ cups milk

450 ml/1¾ cups double/heavy cream

1 vanilla pod/bean, split lengthways

5 UK large/US extra-large eggs

100 g/½ cup sugar

grated zest/peel of 1 lemon

2 tablespoons unsalted butter

8 slices of brioche

6–8 ready-to-eat dried apricots, chopped

a sprinkling of brown sugar, for topping

APRICOT PURÉE:

250 g/9 oz. pitted fresh apricots

freshly squeezed juice of 1 lemon

100 g/½ cup sugar, or more to taste

1 tablespoon apricot brandy or brandy

SERVES 4–6

Butter the slow cooker dish (or 4–6 individual ramekins if your model will accommodate them.)

To make the custard, put the milk and cream in a large saucepan. Use the tip of a small knife to scrape the vanilla seeds directly into the pan. Bring to the boil. Put the eggs and sugar in a large bowl and whisk until frothy. Whisk the milk mixture into the eggs and stir in the lemon zest/peel.

Lightly butter the brioche. Arrange half the brioche, buttered side up, in the slow cooker. Sprinkle half the chopped apricots over the top. Pour the custard over the top, letting it soak into the brioche. Sprinkle with the remaining apricots, top with the rest of the brioche and gently pour in the remaining custard.

Cover with the lid and cook on LOW for 3 hours, until the custard is just set but still slightly wobbly.

Meanwhile, to make the apricot purée, put the fresh apricots in a saucepan, add the lemon juice, sugar, brandy and 4 tablespoons of cold water and simmer for about 10–15 minutes, until the fruit has softened. Transfer to a blender and purée until smooth. The amount of water will depend on how juicy the fruits are — if the purée looks too thick, add a little more.

Remove the dish from the slow cooker, sprinkle with the brown sugar and cook under a preheated grill/broiler, until the top caramelizes to a golden brown. Serve with the apricot purée.

coffee hazelnut cakes with coffee bean sauce

60 g/2 oz. shelled hazelnuts

60 g/½ cup self-raising/rising flour

½ teaspoon baking powder

a pinch of salt

120 g/1 stick unsalted butter, softened

120 g/½ cup brown sugar

finely grated zest/peel of 1 orange

2 teaspoons liquid instant coffee

2 eggs, beaten

COFFEE BEAN SAUCE:

225 g/1 cup sugar

125 ml/½ cup freshly-brewed strong black coffee

5 tablespoons double/heavy cream

TO SERVE (OPTIONAL):

a few coffee beans

1–2 tablespoons malt whisky

candied orange zest/peel

4 individual heatproof bowls, 150 ml/⅔ cup capacity each, buttered and base-lined with baking parchment

SERVES 4

Coffee and hazelnuts make a delicious marriage of flavours and work perfectly here in this indulgent, grown-up dessert.

Put the hazelnuts into a blender and grind until chunky. Transfer to a bowl, then stir in the flour, baking powder and salt.

Put the butter, sugar, orange zest/peel and coffee into a second bowl and beat until light and fluffy. Gradually whisk the eggs into the mixture. Carefully fold in the flour mixture until evenly mixed. It should have a soft dropping consistency. Divide the batter between the prepared bowls, cover with buttered foil, and place in the slow cooker. Pour in enough boiling water to come halfway up the sides of the bowls. Cover with the lid and cook on HIGH for 1½–2 hours, until risen and firm to the touch.

Meanwhile, to make the coffee bean sauce, put the sugar in a saucepan, add 5 tablespoons of cold water and dissolve over low heat. As the liquid becomes clear, increase the heat and bring to the boil. Cook, without stirring, until the sugar forms a golden caramel. Remove from the heat and carefully pour over the coffee (the caramel will splutter, so protect your hand with a cloth.) Return to the heat and add the cream. Continue stirring until smooth, then simmer until reduced to a coating consistency. Remove from the heat. Add the coffee beans and whisky to taste.

Run a small knife around the cakes and turn out carefully onto serving plates. Pour the sauce over the top before serving.

caramel custard

These little French custards make the perfect ending to any meal. Preparation is simple but there are a few tricks to facilitate unmolding. Let the custards sit for 15 minutes before removing them to cool completely. This allows the custard to settle and solidify, making it easier to turn out. Next, dip the base of the moulds in boiling water for 10 seconds, loosen the top of the custard with a fingertip, then turn out onto plates.

450 ml/1¾ cups whole milk

1 vanilla pod/bean, split lengthways

115 g/½ cup plus 2 tablespoons sugar

a pinch of salt

2 eggs

4 ramekins

SERVES 4

Put the milk and vanilla pod/bean in a saucepan and bring to the boil. Immediately remove from the heat, cover and let stand.

To make the caramel, put 75 g/¼ cup of the sugar, the salt and 3 tablespoons of cold water in a small, heavy-based saucepan. Heat until the sugar turns a deep caramel colour, then remove from the heat. When it stops sizzling, pour carefully into the ramekins. Take care not to let the caramel come into contact with your skin as it is very hot. Set the ramekins in the slow cooker and add enough cold water to come halfway up the sides.

Add the remaining sugar to the saucepan of warm milk and stir until dissolved. Remove the vanilla pod/bean and scrape the seeds into the mixture using the tip of a small sharp knife.

Crack the eggs into another bowl and whisk until smooth. Pour the warm vanilla milk into the eggs and stir well. Ladle into the ramekins. Cover each ramekin with foil, then cover with the slow cooker lid and cook on LOW for 2–2½ hours.

Serve at room temperature or chilled either in their ramekins or inverted onto a rimmed plate in a pool of caramel sauce.

pear and chocolate dessert cake

A sophisticated-looking dessert cake that is really easy to make. Any fresh, ripe orchard fruit can be used, but pears are particularly good with chocolate.

3 pears, peeled, cored and halved

100 g/7 tablespoons unsalted butter, softened

100 g/½ cup sugar

40 g/¼ cup ground almonds

2 eggs

100 g/1 cup self-raising/rising flour

30 g/2 heaping tablespoons unsweetened cocoa powder

1 teaspoon baking powder

75 ml/¼ cup milk

a little icing/confectioners' sugar, for dusting

whipped cream, to serve (optional)

SERVES 6

Arrange the pears in the base of a well buttered slow cooker dish.

Put the butter and sugar in a bowl and cream until smooth. Add the ground almonds and eggs and beat well. Sift in the flour, cocoa and baking powder, then fold the mixture together. Add the milk and beat until smooth. Cover the pears with the mixture and level the surface with the back of a spoon.

Cover with the slow cooker lid. Cook on HIGH for about 1 hour 50 minutes, until the sponge springs back when pressed lightly in the centre.

Dust the cake with icing/confectioners' sugar and serve with cream.

white chocolate fondue with gin

75 ml/¼ cup double/heavy cream

3 tablespoons gin

225 g/8 oz. best-quality white chocolate, chopped

TO SERVE:

500 g/2 cups strawberries

250 g/1 cup blueberries

small sweet cookies suitable for dipping, such as ladyfingers, madeleines, langues de chat or amaretti

SERVES 4–6

This delicious fondue makes a change from the more traditional milk or dark chocolate version.

Put the cream and gin in a heatproof bowl (making sure the bowl will fit inside your slow cooker) and whisk together. Top with the chopped chocolate, do not stir, then sit the bowl in the base of the slow cooker. Carefully pour in enough cold water to come halfway up the sides of the bowl and ensuring no water splashes into the chocolate bowl. Cover with the lid then cook on HIGH for 3 hours, without removing the lid.

Wash the strawberries, but do not hull them, then pat them dry with paper towels (if you hull them before washing, they will fill with water.)

Thread a few blueberries onto small skewers. Arrange the blueberry skewers, strawberries and cookies on a serving plate.

Remove the bowl from the slow cooker and, using a small whisk, give the mixture a good whisk to combine the ingredients and give you a smooth chocolate fondue.

Transfer to a fondue pot and set over its tabletop burner, then serve with the fruit and cookies for dipping.

There are many varieties of pumpkin and this recipe can be used to preserve all of them. Make sure that the flesh is firm and not stringy, or it will spoil the finished texture of the chutney. If you are making large quantities, do chop the vegetables in a food processor. You can also use other vegetables such as marrow, courgettes/zucchini, aubergine/eggplant, unripe melons and green tomatoes.

400 g/14 oz. peeled and seeded firm pumpkin or butternut squash flesh, cut into 1-cm/½-inch cubes

200 g/7 oz. ripe tomatoes, skinned, seeded, and chopped

200 g/7 oz. onions, chopped

25 g/2 heaping tablespoons sultanas/golden raisins

250 g/1 scant cup Demerara sugar

1 teaspoon salt

3-cm/1-inch piece of fresh ginger, peeled and finely chopped

1 garlic clove, finely chopped

freshly grated nutmeg, to taste

200 ml/¾ cup malt vinegar

*a large sealable jar
(about 500 g/1 lb.)*

MAKES 1 LARGE JAR

pumpkin and red tomato chutney

Put all the ingredients in the slow cooker. Cook on HIGH for 7 hours, stirring from time to time. Remove the lid and cook 1 further hour. The chutney should be dark, dense and rich. Add extra vinegar if the chutney dries out too much while cooking.

Transfer to a hot sterilized jar (see note below), cover the surface of the chutney with waxed paper, and seal at once. Store for 1–6 months in a cool, dark place before opening. Keep in the fridge once opened.

Note: To sterilize preserving jars, wash them in hot, soapy water and rinse in boiling water. Place in a large saucepan and cover with hot water. Cover and bring the water to the boil and continue boiling for 15 minutes. Turn off the heat, leave the jars in the hot water until just before they are to be filled. Invert the jars onto paper towels to dry. Sterilize the lids for 5 minutes, by boiling. Jars should be filled and sealed while they are still hot.

squash and aubergine chutney

900 g/2 lbs. prepared orange-fleshed squash or pumpkin, cut into 1-cm/½-inch dice

2 large aubergine/eggplants (about 500 g/1 lb.) cut into 1-cm/½-inch dice

650 g/1½ lbs. onions, chopped

4 garlic cloves, crushed

2–3 fresh red chillies/chiles, seeded and thinly sliced or chopped

1 tablespoon each crushed coriander seeds and brown mustard seeds

finely shredded zest/peel and freshly squeezed juice of 1 orange

50 g/2-inch piece of fresh ginger

400 ml/1⅔ cups cider vinegar or white wine vinegar

2 teaspoons salt, plus extra to taste

400 g/2 cups sugar, warmed

cayenne pepper or chilli/chili powder, to taste

a small piece of muslin/cheesecloth

kitchen twine

4–5 medium sealable jars (about 350-g/12-oz. each)

MAKES 4–5 MEDIUM JARS

This is a golden chutney flecked with the dark purple of the aubergine/eggplant and the red of the chillies/chile peppers. Serve it with bread and cheese, with ham and cured meats, or spread thickly to spice up any sandwich. It will keep unopened for at least 12 months in a dark, cool place. Keep in the fridge.

Put the squash and aubergine/eggplants in a large, stainless steel saucepan with the onions, garlic, chillies/chiles, crushed coriander and mustard seeds, and the orange zest/peel and juice. Bash the ginger with a rolling pin to bruise it, tie it in a piece of muslin/cheesecloth, and bury it in the mixture. Pour over the vinegar.

Bring to the boil, transfer the ingredients to the slow cooker, cover with the lid, and cook on HIGH for 4 hours. Remove the lid, add the salt and warmed sugar, stir well to dissolve the sugar and cook for 1 further hour without the lid to reduce the liquid.

It is ready when a wooden spoon drawn over the base of the pan leaves a clear channel for a few seconds. Adjust the seasoning to taste with salt, cayenne, or chili powder. Leave for 10 minutes, stir well, discard the ginger and then transfer to hot, sterilized jars (see note on page 229). Seal immediately, then invert. Let cool before turning the right way up.

Store in a cool, dark place for at least 4 weeks before using. Once open, store in the fridge.

apple, red onion and dried cherry chutney

3 eating apples, such as Golden Delicious, peeled, cored and diced

1 large or 2 medium red onions, halved and sliced

175 g/1 heaping cup dried sour cherries

200 g/¾ cup cider vinegar

150 g/¾ cup light brown sugar

¼ teaspoon ground cloves

¼ teaspoon sea salt

freshly ground black pepper

MAKES 500–750 ML/2–3 CUPS

This sweet chutney works very well with chicken, turkey and even duck, or enjoy it with cheese.

In a large non-reactive saucepan, combine the apples, onion, dried cherries, vinegar, sugar, cloves, salt and a few grinds of black pepper. Transfer everything to the slow cooker, cover with the lid, and cook on HIGH for 6–7 hours, until thick.

Transfer the chutney to a spotlessly clean and dry, sealable airtight container. It will keep in the fridge for up to 2 weeks.

apple, pear and ginger chutney

3 eating apples, such as Golden Delicious, peeled, cored, and diced

2 large ripe pears, peeled, cored and diced

1 large white onion, finely chopped

275 ml/1 cup cider vinegar

350 g/1½ cups plus 2 tablespoons light brown sugar

100 g/½ cup sultanas/golden raisins or raisins

140-g/5 oz. piece of fresh ginger, peeled and finely chopped

½ teaspoon sea salt

½ teaspoon chilli/hot red pepper flakes

MAKES ABOUT 1 LITRE/4 CUPS

This spicy chutney is especially suited to pork and makes a nice sandwich ingredient.

Place the apples, pears, onion, vinegar, sugar, golden raisins, ginger, salt and chilli/pepper flakes in the slow cooker, cover with the lid, and cook on HIGH for 2 hours.

Remove the lid and cook for a further 1–1½ hours to allow the chutney to thicken.

Transfer the chutney to a spotlessly clean and dry, sealable airtight container. It will keep in the fridge for up to 2 weeks.

finely grated zest/peel and freshly squeezed juice of 2 large lemons

125 g/1 stick unsalted butter, cubed

180 g/1 cup sugar

3 eggs, beaten

2 small sealable jars (about 225 g/8 oz. each)

MAKES 2 SMALL JARS

lemon curd

This is a quintessentially British preserve, tart with lemon yet sweet and buttery at the same time. It is delicious spread on toast or on freshly made scones or bread and also an excellent filling for tarts, pound cakes or meringues. Small jars make a great gift. It is very easy to make and will keep for up to 2 weeks in the fridge.

Melt the butter in a saucepan. Add the lemon juice, zest/peel and sugar. Stir until the sugar has dissolved and let cool.

Whisk the eggs into the mixture, strain, and pour into a 1-litre/1-quart heatproof bowl. Cover with foil.

Put the bowl in the slow cooker and add boiling water to come halfway up the side of the bowl. Cover with the lid and cook on LOW for 3–4 hours, until thick. Stir thoroughly.

For a very smooth preserve, push the curd through a fine sieve/strainer, then spoon it into small, hot sterilized jars (see note on page 229). Cover with clingfilm/plastic wrap or waxed paper when cold and seal. Store in the fridge for up to 2 weeks.

index

recipe credits

Sonia Stevenson
braised lamb shanks
    with orange and
    marmalade
chicken and sweet
    potatoes with honey,
    soy and lemon
chicken tagine with
    quinces and
    preserved lemons
choucroute garnie
creamy Greek lemon
    chicken
creole duck
Greek braised lamb
    with okra
Irish carbonnade
la bourride
Lancashire hotpot
lemon chicken with
    dumplings
navarin of lamb
oxtail in red wine
Provençal daube of beef
red-cooked pork
slow cooker stock
steak and kidney
    pudding
Tuscan pork and bean
    casserole
Vietnamese beef
Yankee pot roast

Ross Dobson
beef daube
garlic and chilli rice
    soup with spring
    greens
lamb kefta meatballs
lamb shanks in red
    wine with cannellini
    beans
mushroom and thyme
    ragù with hand-torn
    pasta
root vegetable ragù
    with spiced couscous
Scotch broth
shellfish, tomato and
    couscous stew
slow-cooked onion and
    cider soup
smoky bean hotpot
spiced Muscat figs
winter vegetable
    tagine

Fran Warde
beef and carrot
    casserole with
    cheese dumplings
chicken and bacon pot
chicken soup
chili con carne
classic minestrone
eggs cocotte
golden butternut
    squash soup
meatloaf with tomato
    sauce
pear and chocolate
    cake
prawn curry

Laura Washburn
apple, pear and ginger
    chutney
apple, red onion, and
    dried cherry chutney
beef rolls with cured
    ham in tomato sauce
braised pork chops
    with tomato, orange,
    and chilli
caramel custard
chicken, sausage and
    rice
meatballs in red
    pepper sauce
Portuguese lamb stew
    with piri piri

Fiona Smith
beef and ale pâté
blue cheese fondue
pork, fennel and
    spinach terrine
ratatouille
vacherine fondue with
    caramelized shallots
white chocolate fondue
    with lemon and gin

Fiona Beckett
coq au vin
duck casserole with
    red wine, cinnamon,
    and olives
lamb shanks with red
    wine, rosemary and
    garlic
osso buco-style veal
    chops

Tessa Bramley
apricot bread and
    butter pudding
baked lemon dessert
    with lemon butter
    sauce
blueberry and cherry
    sponge
coffee hazelnut
    cakes with coffee
    bean sauce

Maxine Clark
cassoulet
Mexican pork and
    beans in red chilli
    sauce
smoked and fresh
    salmon terrine
spinach and ricotta
    timbales

Silvana Franco
Italian pasta and bean
    soup
Italian steak sauce
pancetta and turkey
    meatballs
rich Bolognese sauce

Brian Glover
lemon curd
lemon, fennel and
    mushroom risotto
squash and aubergine
    chutney

Rachael Anne Hill
bag-cooked chicken
    with runner beans
baked apples with
    blackberries and
    port sauce
chicken and barley
    braise
prawn and butter bean
    rice

Sunil Vijayakar
beef and pea curry
beef madras
butter chicken
lamb rogan josh

Liz Franklin
lamb and butternut
    squash stew
tagliatelle with rich
    meat sauce

**Manisha Gambhir
Harkins**
Burmese pork hinleh
chickpea soup with
    chorizo, paprika and
    saffron
red-cooked chicken legs

Tonia George
chicken and lentil curry
lamb and broad bean
    tagine
peaches poached in
    vanilla honey syrup

Jennifer Joyce
chunky diner-style chili
three-cheese macaroni
maple baked beans

Caroline Marson
chicken jalfrezi
Mediterranean chunky
    fish stew with
    cheese toasts
Spanish sausage and
    butter bean casserole

**Elsa Petersen-
Schepelern**
butternut and
    courgette pulao
spicy chicken curry
    with butternut and
    spinach
stuffed squash with
    pesto and mozzarella

Ursula Ferrigno
potato, basil and green
    bean risotto
risotto with cannellini
    beans

Ghillie Basan
Moroccan fish stew

Clare Gordon-Smith
tomato and garlic soup

Lindy Wildsmith
pumpkin and red
    tomato chutney

**Jane Milton
(Not Just Food Ltd)**
slow cooker know-how
    (introduction)

picture credits

Key: ph= photographer, a=above, b=below, r=right,
l=left, c=center

Page 6:
Image courtesy of
Cuisinart: Cuisinart
Cook & Hold slow
cooker. Call Cuisinart
on 1-800-211-9604 or
visit www.cuisinart.com
for further information.

Page 7:
Image courtesy of
Crock-Pot®—the
original slow cooker
brand. Visit
www.crockpot.com for
further information.

Caroline Arber
Pages 14al, 14bl, 14br,
23, 27, 48, 55, 59, 127,
132, 166al, 168, 206bl,
224

Martin Brigdale
Pages 11, 45, 56, 93,
166bl, 179, 180bl, 194,
197, 205, 223, 226

Peter Cassidy
Page 2, 8, 20, 44, 47,
50al, 50ar, 65, 82 inset,
102, 120, 121, 130bl,
130br, 142, 144, 150
inset, 151, 166ar, 172,
177 inset, 204 inset,
206al, 206br, 209, 217,
222, 225 both, 231,
232, 233

Nicki Dowey
Pages 1, 160, 163, 176,
210–211

Tara Fisher
Pages 49, 78 inset, 184,
228

Christine Hanscomb
Pages 215, 216, 219, 220

Richard Jung
Pages 14ar, 16, 17, 18,
22, 24, 26, 28, 31, 33b,
69, 81, 95, 97, 98, 103,
138, 165 inset, 166br,
175, 180al, 180br, 186,
188 inset, 189, 190, 193,
196 background, 198,
203, 213, 229, 234, 235

Lisa Linder
Pages 117, 128, 129

William Lingwood
Page 9, 10 both, 19, 34,
36–37, 38–39, 40, 43,
50br, 52–53, 60, 63, 64, 65
inset, 66–67, 68, 71, 72,
75, 76, 78–79 main, 80, 83,
112, 115, 116, 119, 130ar,
135, 136, 139, 140–141,
143, 155, 156, 158–159,
170–171 main, 187, 191,
206ar, 210 inset, 227

Jason Lowe
Pages, 180ar, 182–183,
185

James Merrell
Page 32

Diana Miller
Pages 33a, 105 inset,
199 inset

David Montgomery
Page 214

David Munns
Pages 4, 84, 87, 88, 91,
92, 152, 196 inset

Noel Murphy
Pages 123, 124

William Reavell
Page 12, 104, 148, 170
inset, 208

Yuki Sugiura
Pages 5, 25

Debi Treloar
Pages 113, 164, 201,
202, 221

Pia Tryde
Page 70

Ian Wallace
Page 35

Kate Whitaker
Pages 30, 42, 50bl, 57,
74, 82 background, 89,
96, 99, 100, 101, 105
background, 107, 108,
109, 111, 130al, 134, 146,
147, 150 background,
162, 165 background,
169, 174, 177
background, 188
background, 199
background, 204
background, 212, 230